STANLEY NEWMAN's
SITCOM
CROSSWORDS

**Random House
Puzzles & Games**

ISBN: 0-8129-3469-5

Random House Puzzles & Games Web site address:
www.puzzlesatrandom.com

Manufactured in the United States of America

2 4 6 8 9 7 5 3

First Edition

INTRODUCTION

Welcome to *Sitcom Crosswords*, a puzzle book that celebrates 50 of the most popular sitcoms of all time. As far as we know, this is the first crossword book whose themes are devoted exclusively to situation comedies.

Each puzzle covers a different series. Alphabetically (as they are presented herein), they range from *The Addams Family* to *The Wonder Years*; chronologically, from *Our Miss Brooks* to *Friends*. To enhance your solving enjoyment, each puzzle includes the sitcom's setting and some interesting trivia. If you're a fan of trivia in general, I commend to your attention the Random House book *10,000 Answers: The Ultimate Trivia Encyclopedia*, coauthored by yours truly, in which many of these facts first appeared.

As a bonus, you'll find many other clues in each puzzle related to sitcoms and TV, in addition to the "theme" clues. I hope you'll be pleasantly surprised at how much "TV stuff" there is throughout. The entertainment-filled crosswords I've been creating for *People* magazine for the past ten years have been good training for *Sitcom Crosswords*.

For their help in the preparation of this book, I would like to thank these Random House folks:

- Sheryl Stebbins, my publisher
- Sandy Fein, my editor, for her many helpful suggestions and good counsel
- Jon Delfin, for his thorough proofreading of the manuscript

Your comments on any aspect of *Sitcom Crosswords* are most welcome. You can reach me via regular mail or e-mail at the addresses below.

If you're on e-mail, I invite you to join "Fans of Stan," a free service that will keep you abreast of my activities in the puzzle world: when new books of mine are published, seminars and tournaments I'm conducting, etc. Simply e-mail me at StanXwords @aol.com.

Best wishes for happy solving!

Stan Newman

Regular mail: P.O. Box 69, Massapequa Park, NY 11762
(Please enclose a self-addressed stamped envelope if you'd like a reply.)

E-mail: StanXwords@aol.com

1 THE ADDAMS FAMILY

000 Cemetery Lane, Cemetery Ridge, U.S.A.

ACROSS

1 Stare at
5 Monty Hall offering
9 Morita of *Happy Days*
12 Chimney dirt
13 Wheel connector
14 Actress Thurman
15 Hairy relative on the show
17 Fitness center
18 "__ was saying . . ."
19 Jack Sprat's no-no
20 Vehicle for Kramden
22 Oboes and bassoons
24 *Buffy the Vampire Slayer* star
27 Harrelson of *Cheers*
30 Singer Horne
31 Writer Angelou
34 Former Mideast alliance: Abbr.
35 Greek god story, for example
36 Donahue of *Hawaiian Eye*
37 *The Mary Tyler Moore Show* spinoff
39 Pepé Le Pew and family
41 Potts of *Designing Women*
45 __ Speedwagon
46 Sabrina's Salem, for one
48 Terre Haute's state: Abbr.
49 Fitness center
51 Gomez Addams portrayer
54 Coop dweller
55 Came in for a landing
56 *Baywatch* star __ Lee Nolin
57 Mork's spaceship
58 Susan Lucci character
59 Sounds of reproach

DOWN

1 Felix Unger's roommate
2 Duck's cousin
3 Danny, on *Taxi*
4 Little green men: Abbr.
5 *X-Files* investigator
6 Leave the building
7 Computer keyboard key
8 Leave alone
9 Son on the show
10 Brenneman of *NYPD Blue*
11 Scottish cap
16 In that case
21 *The Tracey __ Show*
23 Dobie Gillis portrayer Hickman
24 Greek sandwich
25 Picnic pest
26 Football cheer
28 Yours and mine
29 Morse code sound
31 Rockies and Andes: Abbr.
32 Noah's creation
33 Lurch's catchphrase on the show
38 *Star Trek: The Next Generation* character
40 Savalas cop series
42 Evenings, on marquees
43 How contracts should be signed
44 Dame Everage et al.
46 Jay Leno's prominent feature
47 Poker ritual
49 That woman
50 *Married . . . With Children* mom
52 Suffix for scram
53 Bilko's rank: Abbr.

2 THE ADVENTURES OF OZZIE AND HARRIET

822 Sycamore Road, Hillsdale, California

ACROSS

1 Basketball great Chamberlain
5 Assist
8 Mardi __
12 Get an __ effort
13 Double-helix molecule
14 Take a chance
15 The two kids on the show
18 *Tonight* host before Jack
19 New England college, for short
20 Under the weather
22 Thickness
23 Perlman of *Cheers*
26 Perry Mason creator __ Stanley Gardner
28 __ Paulo, Brazil
31 Alma mater of 15 Across
34 Wise bird
35 "__ Misbehavin'"
36 Agenda element
37 Medicine dosages: Abbr.
38 Fastest passenger plane: Abbr.
40 God of the Moslems
43 __'s *Company*
47 The show's prime-time run
51 Concerning
52 Capture
53 Beef cut
54 Film holder
55 And so on: Abbr.
56 Enthusiasm

DOWN

1 Big bankrolls
2 "__ first you don't succeed . . ."
3 *The __ Boat*
4 __ Pursuit (board game and game show)
5 Dentists' organization: Abbr.
6 *Newhart* setting
7 What 15 Across call Ozzie
8 Very dirty
9 Costa __
10 Poses a question
11 "The __ the limit!"
16 Neighbor of Penn.
17 Made a courtroom decision
21 Emmanuel of *Webster*
22 Sitcom storylines
23 Greek letter
24 In what way
25 Kay follower
27 TV Tarzan Ely
28 Take a rest
29 Mature
30 Electrical unit
32 Tycoon's ship
33 Boom Boom's catchphrase on *Welcome Back, Kotter*
37 *The Brady Bunch* mom
39 Pigpen
40 From a distance
41 Finish second
42 Troubadour's instrument
44 Actor Julia
45 Columnist Bombeck
46 Sports cable channel
48 Compass point: Abbr.
49 Have dinner
50 *Friends* network

3 ALL IN THE FAMILY

704 Hauser Street, Queens, New York

ACROSS

1 New Deal agency: Abbr.
4 Wild guess
8 Russian ruler of old
12 Junk dealer, for Fred Sanford
13 Item of Japanese cuisine
14 Actor Cronyn
15 Rob Reiner's role on the show
18 *The Price Is Right* action
19 Author Deighton
20 Early American fur magnate
23 36 Across' nickname for 41 Across
27 Flower parts
28 Medical-show workers: Abbr.
29 Vitamin recommendation: Abbr.
30 __ Raider (Lara Croft video game)
31 *Soupy Sales Show* projectile
32 In the near future
33 Taylor of *The $1.98 Beauty Show*
34 Anger
35 Former German money, for short
36 Archie Bunker portrayer
38 Office assistants
39 Dog-registry organization: Abbr.
40 Chicago's state: Abbr.
41 Edith Bunker portrayer
48 Hoss Cartwright's real first name
49 *Born Free* lioness
50 Yoko __
51 *What's My Line?* host
52 Ocho __, Jamaica
53 Encountered

DOWN

1 Ted Baxter's TV station
2 Luau side dish
3 *Dharma & Greg* network
4 Elevator alternative
5 __ the line (behaved)
6 CIO's partner
7 Jackie Gleason's sitcom employer
8 *Addams Family* servant
9 Large family vehicle: Abbr.
10 French friend
11 VCR button
16 Nuclear weapon, for short
17 Wallet fillers
20 The Jetsons' dog
21 Keeping a stiff upper lip
22 Musical pace
23 Not as humid
24 Wide
25 Like a lot
26 Armored vehicles
31 __ and Gamble (frequent TV sponsor)
32 Funt's order
34 Printer's purchases
35 J.R. Ewing's headquarters
37 Walker of *Rhoda*
40 __ facto
41 Pa Clampett
42 Historical period
43 Feel poorly
44 __ Baba
45 Magnum portrayer Selleck
46 Early afternoon
47 "I should say __!"

1	2	3		4	5	6	7		8	9	10	11
12				13					14			
15			16					17				
			18				19					
20	21	22				23				24	25	26
27						28				29		
30					31				32			
33				34				35				
36			37					38				
			39				40					
41	42	43				44				45	46	47
48					49					50		
51					52					53		

4 THE ANDY GRIFFITH SHOW

Mayberry, 34 Across

ACROSS

1 Young fellow
4 Shoemakers' tools
8 Pioneering sitcom of 1949–56
12 Actress MacGraw
13 She was Carla on *Cheers*
14 Newspaper page
15 Opie's real first name, today
16 Barney Fife portrayer on the show
18 *The Donna Reed Show* family name
20 Portion of corn
21 Concludes
24 Della of *Touched by an Angel*
28 Hawkeye Pierce portrayer
31 Dressed
33 Go bad
34 Setting of the show
37 Open-slot schedule abbreviation
38 Utah resort
39 "Meet Me __ Louis"
40 Radar O'Reilly, for one
42 Greek letters
44 Single-helix molecule
46 Fran Drescher's TV occupation
50 He played Goober Pyle's brother on the show
55 Fuss
56 Brainstorm
57 Dagwood's bratty neighbor
58 Carryall
59 Memorable Henry Winkler role
60 Where Nashville is: Abbr.
61 Something to do at 38 Across

DOWN

1 Phyllis' husband on *The Mary Tyler Moore Show*
2 Considerably
3 TV roast host, familiarly
4 *Our Miss Brooks* star
5 __ *Do You Trust?* (Johnny Carson game show)
6 Football great Dawson
7 "For Pete's __!"
8 TV's Lone Ranger
9 Likely
10 Encountered
11 Words from the sponsor
17 Marilu Henner, on *Taxi*
19 Like Felix Unger
22 750, in Roman numerals
23 Fred Flintstone's boss
25 Moran of *Happy Days*
26 Hoss and Little Joe, to Ben
27 State: Fr.
28 Prefix meaning "against"
29 '80s TV sheriff
30 *Win, Lose or __*
32 Smell __ (be suspicious)
35 Barbera's animation partner
36 Bart's younger sister
41 *I Love Lucy* executive producer
43 Williams of *Happy Days*
45 Aid in a crime
47 Captures
48 Bismarck's state: Abbr.
49 He's "smarter than the average bear"
50 Skippy competitor
51 Bachelor's last words
52 What boys become
53 Grand __ Opry
54 '70s presidential monogram

1	2	3		4	5	6	7		8	9	10	11
12				13					14			
15				16				17				
18			19				20					
			21		22	23		24		25	26	27
28	29	30			31		32			33		
34				35					36			
37				38				39				
40			41			42		43				
			44		45			46		47	48	49
50	51	52				53	54			55		
56				57					58			
59				60					61			

Aunt Bee's full first name was Beatrice.

Andy and Opie's favorite fishing spot was Meyer's Lake.

5 THE BEVERLY HILLBILLIES

518 Crestview Drive, Beverly Hills, California

ACROSS

1 Sitcom with an 11-year prime-time run
5 Environmentally friendly prefix
8 *The King and I* setting
12 Ending for million
13 Short swim
14 Johnson of *Laugh-In*
15 Family surname on the show
17 Study of the Earth: Abbr.
18 Toshiba competitor
19 *Who's the Boss?* star
20 TV antenna alternative
23 Mrs. Roy Rogers
24 *NYPD* __
25 Rachins of *L.A. Law*
27 Male sheep
30 Feeling tense
31 Elly __ (character on the show)
32 Daly of *Cagney & Lacey*
33 Sinking-ship deserter
34 *Friends* character
35 Meal for Mister Ed
36 Takes advantage of
38 Meara and Bancroft
39 The show's network
41 Coleman of *Diff'rent Strokes*
43 Otherwise
44 The title characters' banker
48 Regulation
49 Wide shoe
50 Is obligated to
51 Savage of *The Wonder Years*
52 Where Albany is: Abbr.
53 TV's Batman

DOWN

1 Bub
2 Feel poorly
3 Spanish Mrs.: Abbr.
4 *Amen* star
5 *I Dream of Jeannie* star
6 *Sex and the* __ (HBO series)
7 Make a choice
8 Katey of *Married . . . With Children*
9 Granny portrayer on the show
10 From __ (completely)
11 Prefix for bucks or hit
16 "The Raven" poet
19 Blocker of *Bonanza*
20 Trucker with a transmitter
21 Colleague of Farr and Swit
22 The title characters' hometown
23 __ *of Our Lives* (soap opera)
25 John of *Good Times*
26 __ Vegas
28 Start the pot going
29 *M*A*S*H* meal
32 Wally Cleaver portrayer
34 Gun the engine
37 *The Avengers* character
38 __ *gratia artis* (MGM motto)
39 *What's My Line?* regular
40 Something hard to see
41 Sue Ellen Ewing portrayer
42 Roll-call votes
44 Family room
45 Feeling of wonder
46 *WKRP* newsman Nessman
47 Massachusetts clock setting: Abbr.

1	2	3	4		5	6	7		8	9	10	11
12					13				14			
15				16					17			
			18					19				
20	21	22					23					
24					25	26				27	28	29
30					31				32			
33				34					35			
		36	37					38				
39	40					41	42					
43					44				45	46	47	
48					49				50			
51					52				53			

6 BEWITCHED

1164 Morning Glory Circle, Westport, Connecticut

ACROSS

1 450, in Roman numerals
4 Story line
8 Not working, as a battery
12 __ G. Carroll of *Topper*
13 *The West Wing* star
14 Gray of *Buck Rogers in the 25th Century*
15 McHale's employer: Abbr.
16 Dotty relative on the show
18 __ *Is Enough* ('70s sitcom)
20 Chair or stool
21 WB Network owner
23 Friend of Richie and Potsie
27 Have coming
30 *The Clan of the Cave Bear* author
33 Gabor of *Green Acres*
34 Nosy neighbor on the show
37 __-Wan Kenobi
38 Software buyer
39 Simple
40 Sabrina's talking cat
42 Foster Brooks persona
44 Alphabetic quartet
47 Walter Lantz toon
51 Darrin's boss on the show
55 Actress Carrere
56 Dean Martin's home state
57 At what time
58 Politically unaffiliated: Abbr.
59 Tabitha, on the show
60 Calendar abbreviation
61 __ *Hunt* (Lloyd Bridges series)

DOWN

1 Find for Columbo
2 Lucie Arnaz's dad
3 *Nanny and the Professor* star
4 Dana of *Diff'rent Strokes*
5 Mary Richards' boss
6 Possesses
7 Head: Fr.
8 Burke of *Designing Women*
9 Significant period
10 Run on TV
11 Gene splicer's concern
17 *Cheers* waitress
19 Martin Landau, on *Mission: Impossible*
22 Scottish girl
24 *Star Wars* princess
25 Army recruits: Abbr.
26 Not at all clear
27 Swelled heads
28 Jessica of *Dark Angel*
29 Thin as a __
31 Arthur Godfrey's instrument
32 Goes wrong
35 Delicious
36 Presidential power
41 Youngest of the Jetsons
43 *Laugh-In* announcer
45 Canned-food label abbreviation
46 McGarrett's island
48 Mayberry tippler
49 Eat well
50 *Seinfeld* conversation filler
51 Tennis shot
52 Cry of discovery
53 Bit of barbecue
54 Golf platform

1	2	3		4	5	6	7		8	9	10	11
12				13					14			
15				16			17					
18			19			20						
			21		22			23		24	25	26
27	28	29			30	31	32			33		
34				35				36				
37				38			39					
40			41				42	43				
			44		45	46		47		48	49	50
51	52	53				54				55		
56				57						58		
59				60						61		

7 THE BOB NEWHART SHOW

Lake Shore Drive, Chicago, Illinois

ACROSS

1 JFK's successor
4 *The Winds of __* ('83 miniseries)
7 First name of 34 Across on the show
12 Actress Leoni
13 Tempe school: Abbr.
14 Sports stadium
15 Jerry Robinson's occupation on the show
17 *Our Gang* dog
18 Talk
19 Pronoun for a ship
21 Infant's neckwear
23 Comedian who had a '93-'94 sitcom
28 Sixth sense
31 Etta of the comics
33 Corporal Klinger portrayer
34 She was 54 Across' receptionist on the show
37 "How sweet __!"
38 Comedian Rudner
39 Compass point: Abbr.
40 The Ewings and the Barneses

42 Zsa Zsa's sister
44 Occupation ending
46 Georgia of *The Mary Tyler Moore Show*
50 Tony Randall's sitcom character
54 The title star's role on the show
56 Pottery fragment
57 Very long time
58 Coffee brewer
59 Shelley Long's successor on *Cheers*
60 *Cheers* serving
61 Heavy weight

DOWN

1 British corporations: Abbr.
2 Road Runner's sound
3 Curtin of *Saturday Night Live*
4 Frequent *Magnum, p.i.* setting
5 Beast of burden
6 Buzzi of *Laugh-In*
7 Italian isle
8 Exist
9 On a pension: Abbr.
10 *__ Day at a Time*

11 Install, as carpeting
16 '60s heartthrob Hunter
20 John Beresford Tipton's Silverstone, e.g.
22 Amanda of *Married . . . With Children*
24 Gridiron group: Abbr.
25 Sheep sounds
26 Curved lines
27 *The __ Carey Show*
28 Give off
29 Satisfy fully
30 Grand __ auto race
32 Prefix for light
35 Civil War side: Abbr.
36 Penny Marshall sitcom role
41 Like Steve Urkel
43 Industrious insect
45 Mrs. Danny DeVito
47 Overabundance
48 Architect Saarinen
49 Vanessa Redgrave's sister
50 *Silk Stalkings* network
51 Boston Bruins' group: Abbr.
52 Guy's date
53 Before, in poems
55 Warner Bros. owner

Emily Hartley (Suzanne Pleshette) taught at the Gorman Elementary School.

The instrumental theme song of the show was "Home to Emily."

Florida Friebus, who portrayed a therapy-group patient, played Dwayne Hickman's mother on The Many Loves of Dobie Gillis.

8 THE BRADY BUNCH

4222 Clinton Avenue, Los Angeles, California

ACROSS

1 Apple Computer competitor
4 Donny of *Happy Days*
8 Silent assents
12 Aussie jumper
13 Neighborhood
14 Home-furnishings chain
15 Two of the Brady kids
18 Adam of *Chicago Hope*
19 Police chief on *Batman*
20 __ and improved
22 *Air Force One*, for one
23 Hazel's occupation
26 Musical work
28 One of the Brady kids
31 Rooney of *60 Minutes*
32 Barney, to Fred
33 Top-rated
34 Scoreboard postings: Abbr.
35 Hirsch/DeVito sitcom
36 Mailed away
37 Get off one's feet
38 Behave
40 *Lost in* __
43 *Spenser: For Hire* star
47 Two of the Brady kids
51 Ken of *thirty-something*
52 Zilch
53 Showed the way
54 Head: Fr.
55 Sherman Hemsley sitcom
56 Poetic preposition

DOWN

1 *My Friend* __ ('50s sitcom)
2 Male pig
3 Mearth's dad
4 Jessica Fletcher's home
5 "Are you a man __ mouse?"
6 Caribbean, for example
7 Brown shade
8 *The Edge of* __ (soap opera)
9 Gumbo ingredient
10 Bambi, for one
11 *The Forsyte* __
16 One of the Brady kids
17 Accomplishes
21 Luke Duke portrayer
22 Diahann Carroll sitcom
23 Tourist's reference
24 Picnic pest
25 Passports and driver's licenses
27 Cable network
28 Rhoda's husband
29 Actress Jillian
30 After taxes
33 The Jetsons' pet
35 Wedding-cake level
37 Sitcom segment
39 Ricky Ricardo was one
40 Notice
41 Brazilian soccer great
42 Take a crack __
44 Suffix for access
45 "Good buddy"
46 David __ Pierce of *Frasier*
48 __-Alicia of *Falcon Crest*
49 *China Beach* setting
50 JFK's predecessor

The family dog was Tiger.

1 2 3 4 5 6 7 8 9 10 11
12 13 14
15 16 17
18 19
20 21 22
23 24 25 26 27 28 29 30
31 32 33
34 35 36
37 38 39
40 41 42 43 44 45 46
47 48 49 50
51 52 53
54 55 56

The kids attended Fillmore Junior High and Westdale High.

Carol Brady's (Florence Henderson's) maiden name was Tyler.

9 CHEERS

112 1/2 Beacon Street, Boston, Massachusetts

ACROSS

1 "And" or "or": Abbr.
5 Female deer
8 Ward Cleaver's wife
12 Herman Melville novel
13 Outrigger implement
14 Physicist's study
15 Shelley Long's role on the show
18 Waters of *Beulah*
19 Put to work
20 *Roget's* entry: Abbr.
22 Bochco legal series
27 Winter month: Abbr.
30 Donaldson's namesakes
33 Prince Charles' game
34 Nicholas Colasanto's role on the show
37 Thailand's former name
38 Letters before W
39 Install a lawn
40 *The Outer Limits* genre
42 Merit-badge organization: Abbr.
44 Clamor
47 Melissa Rivers' dad
51 Rhea Perlman's role on the show
56 Spiny houseplant
57 Language suffix
58 Lincoln or Ford
59 Amanda of *Max Headroom*
60 Guys
61 Most with August birthdays

DOWN

1 Cryptogram key
2 Leave out
3 __ Beery, Jr. of *The Rockford Files*
4 Grandpa of *Hee Haw*
5 "What's up, __?"
6 *Hawaiian Eye* setting
7 Epochs
8 Boxer's punch
9 Western Indian
10 Neither's partner
11 Printing widths
16 *Family Ties* mom
17 Harris of *thirtysomething*
21 Siestas
23 *The Simpsons* shop owner
24 Sports setback
25 In addition
26 Lumber
27 Parker of *Daniel Boone*
28 Newsman Sevareid
29 __ B'rith
31 Bathtub accessory
32 Social slight
35 *Mission: Impossible* group: Abbr.
36 Boob tube
41 Actress Lupino
43 *Let's Make __* (Monty Hall show)
45 Agenda element
46 Durante's claim to fame
48 Mucilage
49 Choir voice
50 Spanish rivers
51 Baseballer's topper
52 Chicken __ king
53 Trigger's rider
54 Bandleader Brown
55 Stimpy's pal

1	2	3	4		5	6	7		8	9	10	11
12					13				14			
15				16				17				
18						19						
			20		21			22	23	24	25	26
27	28	29		30		31	32		33			
34			35					36				
37				38					39			
40			41			42		43				
				44	45	46		47		48	49	50
51	52	53	54			55						
56				57				58				
59				60				61				

10 THE COSBY SHOW

10 Stigwood Avenue, Brooklyn, New York

ACROSS

1 Traffic tie-up
4 Laverne and Shirley lived in one: Abbr.
7 Niles Crane's first wife
12 Source of silver
13 __ de Janeiro
14 *Get Smart* star
15 With 52 Across, school attended by Denise on the show
17 Walker of *Cheyenne*
18 Space shuttle agency: Abbr.
19 Peeples of *Fame*
21 Altar exchanges
22 *Six Feet Under* network
24 Mad scientist's workplace
26 First name of Suzanne Sugarbaker's portrayer
29 __ room
30 When many soap operas air: Abbr.
33 Phylicia Rashad's role on the show
36 Dennis the Menace, for one
37 Bear in a '60s TV series
38 *Peyton Place* star
39 What corporals call sergeants
40 Buenos Aires' country: Abbr.
41 Like a wet noodle
44 Barbara __ Geddes of *Dallas*
46 *Harper Valley P.T.A.* star
50 *The Untouchables* character
52 See 15 Across
54 Concerning
55 Taunting shout
56 Distress signal
57 Mel Blanc's duck voice
58 Courtroom concern
59 Suffix for cartoon

DOWN

1 *Trapper* __, M.D.
2 Pavarotti performance
3 Diner on *Alice*
4 Popeye tattoo site
5 Steve Allen's instrument
6 Singer Braxton
7 Big __ (Whopper alternative)
8 Groucho Marx specialty
9 SWAT-team action
10 __ *Angel* (Mae West film)
11 Fastest passenger planes
16 Christine of *Chicago Hope*
20 *Family Ties* teen
23 Benton of *Hee Haw*
25 James Arness or Eddie Albert
26 601, in Roman numerals
27 Shade tree
28 Once around the track
29 __ *for Your Life* (Ben Gazzara series)
30 Vigoda of *Barney Miller*
31 *The Golden Girls* setting: Abbr.
32 __ Aviv
34 WKRP salesperson
35 Jim Rockford's friend
39 *Get Smart*, for one
40 McGarrett's farewell
41 Principal role
42 *Casablanca* character
43 Annoy
45 Green science: Abbr.
47 Mr. Arnaz
48 Conceits
49 *Empty* __ (Richard Mulligan sitcom)
51 Make an attempt
53 Depressed

The show was honored with a "Celebrate the Century" stamp issued by the U.S. Postal Service.

Cliff Huxtable (Bill Cosby) gave his daughter Rudy (Keshia Knight Pulliam) kisses that he called "zerberts."

Vanessa (Tempestt Bledsoe) attended Lincoln University.

1	2	3		4	5	6		7	8	9	10	11
12				13				14				
15			16					17				
18					19		20		21			
			22	23			24	25				
26	27	28				29				30	31	32
33					34			35				
36				37			38					
			39			40						
41	42	43		44	45			46	47	48	49	
50			51		52	53						
54				55			56					
57				58			59					

11 THE DICK VAN DYKE SHOW

148 Bonnie Meadow Road, New Rochelle, New York

ACROSS

1 Rat-__ (rapping sound)
5 Costar of Ted and Shelley
9 The title star's first name on the show
12 "Goodbye, Columbus" author
13 Holliman of *Police Woman*
14 Conceit
15 Sally and Buddy's occupations on the show
18 Sportscast replay
19 Jobs for Perry Mason
20 Finish
22 Fellows
23 Baseball official
26 "It Ain't Gonna Rain __"
28 Corporal Klinger's memorable feature
32 Producer portrayer on the show
35 Mrs. Oliver Wendell Douglas
36 News article
37 Football scores: Abbr.
38 Merchandise: Abbr.
40 __ *Abner*
42 Walk-on role
45 Mary Tyler Moore's role on the show
49 With *The*, Buddy and Sally's employer
53 Highways: Abbr.
54 Bill Cosby's first TV series
55 One of these days
56 Whole bunch
57 Raison d'__
58 Electrical resistance units

DOWN

1 Curved lines
2 __ *Time* (*Home Improvement* show-within-a-show)
3 Prefix for sphere
4 Henry Mancini wrote it for *Newhart*
5 Alejandro of *The Flying Nun*
6 *Hee* __
7 Make a mistake
8 *The Brady Bunch* housekeeper
9 Roger of *Cheers*
10 Meanie
11 J.D. Hogg's nickname
16 Pescow of *Angie*
17 Urich's *Vega$* role
21 Roberts of *Everybody Loves Raymond*
22 *The Price Is Right* employee
23 Internet address
24 1002, in Roman numerals
25 Some home computers
27 Denver summer clock setting: Abbr.
29 Halloween month: Abbr.
30 Outfield material
31 Parker's rank on *McHale's Navy*: Abbr.
33 Jean of *The Danny Thomas Show*
34 *The Bob Newhart Show* character
39 Maynard G. Krebs' pal
41 Cowboy gear
42 __ Reiner (producer of the show)
43 Actor __ Ray
44 Ship's spar
46 Exclamation of dread
47 __ *222* ('70s TV series)
48 Grain beards
50 Alphabetic trio
51 Rainy month: Abbr.
52 Change the color of

Buddy Sorrell's (Morey Amsterdam's) real first name was Maurice.

45 Across' favorite soap opera was Town of Passion.

9 Across' Army nickname was "Pitter Patter Petrie."

12 F TROOP

Fort Courage, Kansas

ACROSS

1 Christmas Specials month: Abbr.
4 Grant's newspaper
8 Humid
12 Significant time
13 Take the bus
14 Racetrack fence
15 Forrest Tucker's role on the show
18 Gilligan's home
19 Monogram part: Abbr.
20 "The Old __ Picker" (Tennessee Ernie Ford)
21 Clairvoyant's claim
24 *48 Hours* network
26 *Jeopardy!* host before Alex
29 Cube inventor Rubik
31 Allie's friend
35 Trading partners of 15 and 54 Across on the show
38 Shakespeare's river
39 Put away for a rainy day
40 Altitudes: Abbr.
41 *Texaco Star Theater* network
43 Japanese money
45 Molinaro and Martino
48 __ Grande
50 Klinger's home state
54 Larry Storch's role on the show
58 Clumsy one
59 *Maude* producer
60 Bud Abbott's partner
61 Alley's *Cheers* role
62 Start the pot
63 Annapolis graduate: Abbr.

DOWN

1 Actress Moore
2 Greek love god
3 Betz of *The Donna Reed Show*
4 __ la la
5 *The Adventures of __ Tin Tin*
6 David Cassidy, in the '70s
7 *Win, Lose or Draw* host
8 Peter Marshall's sister
9 *Modern Maturity* publisher
10 Archie Bunker's son-in-law
11 Court statement
16 Beaver Cleaver exclamation
17 Sphere
22 Make a dress
23 Presley of *Dallas*
25 Do downhill, perhaps
26 "Eureka!"
27 Clifton Davis' title on *Amen*: Abbr.
28 Boxing result
30 Actress Long
32 Ooh and __
33 Cable network started by Ted Turner
34 Superman's insignia
36 *One Day at a Time* mom
37 Billy __ Williams
42 Family member, for short
44 Eggy drink
45 Paris landmark
46 *Mission: Impossible* composer Schifrin
47 Somers' surname on *Three's Company*
49 Not shuttered
51 Skipper portrayer on *Gilligan's Island*
52 Laundry appliance
53 Burden
55 1950s presidential initials
56 Derby or fedora
57 *You __ There* (Cronkite series)

Wrangler Jane's (Melody Patterson's) real name was Jane Angelica Thrift.

1	2	3		4	5	6	7		8	9	10	11
12				13					14			
15			16					17				
18						19				20		
			21	22	23		24		25			
26	27	28		29		30			31	32	33	34
35			36				37				
38				39				40			
		41	42			43		44			
45	46	47		48		49			50	51	52	53
54			55			56	57				
58				59				60			
61				62				63			

Her horse was named Pecos.

54 Across' horse was Barney.

13 FATHER KNOWS BEST

607 South Maple Street, Springfield, U.S.A.

ACROSS

1 Wide-open mouth sound
4 Connie Brooks portrayer
9 Orson's home planet
12 Swimsuit part
13 Jerry Stiller's missus
14 Boo follower
15 Bud's portrayer on the show
17 "Am __ understand that . . ."
18 Jodie Foster alma mater
19 Young-__ (kids)
20 3rd __ From the Sun
21 Barn bird
23 Australian bird
25 Robert Young, on the show
28 "Go team!"
30 Scratchy's friend on The Simpsons
34 Princess' portrayer on the show
37 Archie Bunker, for one
38 Attorney's degree: Abbr.
39 Quaint hotel
40 Notes of the scale
42 Salon liquid
44 Green Acres setting
47 __ the West Was Won
49 Homer's middle child
53 British brew
54 Mom portrayer on the show
56 Trapper John and Marcus Welby: Abbr.
57 Keats or Shelley
58 Marshal Dillon carried one
59 Have brunch
60 Fellows
61 Yoko __

DOWN

1 L.A. Law character
2 Showcase for a soprano
3 Soaps actress Deidre
4 Judging __ (prime-time series)
5 Actor with a recurring role
6 "Rats!"
7 Clean the blackboard
8 Opposite of aye
9 Cincinnati's state
10 College military program: Abbr.
11 Weirdo
16 Sign of the zodiac
20 Actress Lee
22 Murder, She __
24 Mork's mate
25 Society-page teen
26 __ Baba
27 Work in a mine
29 The "good" cholesterol
31 Greek letter
32 Attila follower
33 Hankering
35 Cheers character
36 Rawhide setting
41 Evening __ (Burt Reynolds sitcom)
43 Tarzan of TV
44 TV series set at a performing arts high school
45 Benjamin Franklin Pierce portrayer
46 Take a breather
48 Getting __ years
50 Othello bad guy
51 Phaser setting
52 __ time (never)
54 Run for health
55 Ounces and pounds: Abbr.

Jim Anderson's (Robert Young's) employer was the General Insurance Company.

54 Across (Margaret Anderson) portrayed Mr. Spock's mother on Star Trek.

Bud's (15 Across') real name was James Anderson, Jr.

14 THE FLINTSTONES

345 Stone Cave Road, Bedrock

ACROSS

1 Dentist's degree: Abbr.
4 Sherilyn of *Twin Peaks*
8 Singer Lane
12 CBS symbol
13 Jordanian, for example
14 *The Avengers* character
15 He voiced Dino and Barney Rubble on the show
17 Ruler of Kuwait
18 Ted Lange, on *The Love Boat*
19 Veronica of *Hill Street Blues*
20 Carl Reiner's kid
22 Accessory for Kookie
23 Artemus Ward's partner
26 Bring up
28 Gorilla or chimp
31 Elevation: Abbr.
32 Fred's wife on the show
33 8 Down star
34 __ de Janeiro
35 Device on a door
36 Andy's friend
37 Midday
39 So far
41 Onetime *Saturday Night Live* regular
43 Esther of *Good Times*
47 Constricting snakes
48 He voiced Fred Flintstone
51 Golden Fleece ship
52 Archie Bunker drove one
53 Shrewish sort
54 Watched on TV
55 Fencing sword
56 Poem of praise

DOWN

1 Bruce Willis ex
2 Textile chemicals
3 Ward of *Sisters*
4 Edie of *The Sopranos*
5 Chapter of history
6 One of the Bobbsey Twins
7 *Seinfeld* network
8 With *The*, '80s action series
9 Betty and Barney's kid
10 French cheese
11 __ Hamner, Jr. (*The Waltons* creator)
16 Bret Maverick's brother
19 Bar mitzvah dance
21 Actor Benben
22 Like TV's *Batman*
23 Armed conflict
24 Actor Wallach
25 Setting for the show
27 Overhead railways
29 PGA member
30 UFO pilots: Abbr.
32 __ *the Boss?*
36 Suffix for comment
38 Actor Bean
40 Bert's friend
41 Graduate degrees: Abbr.
42 Olden days
44 Carson's successor
45 Heavy metal
46 Cutting surface
48 Chowed down
49 Santa Claus perch
50 Lumberjack's tool

15 FRASIER

Eliot Bay Apartments, Seattle, Washington

ACROSS

1 Dollar divisions: Abbr.
4 Letters on a phone
7 '70s talk-show host
12 Gun owners' group: Abbr.
13 *"Now I've got it!"*
14 Earns a living
15 Bob Briscoe's nickname on the show
17 They replaced francs and guilders
18 Actor Romero
19 Prayer conclusion
21 Where Omaha is: Abbr.
23 "Weekend __" (*SNL* segment)
27 Captain Hook's assistant
30 Steak order
32 Author Levin
33 Star of the show
36 Thanksgiving vegetable
37 American alliance: Abbr.
38 Makes a request
39 Pulver's rank
41 Card game
43 Sandwich orders
45 *Lois &* __
49 __ *Luck* (DeLuise sitcom)
52 He portrays Frasier's father
54 Tabitha of MTV
55 Bullfight cheer
56 Prefix for plop
57 "__ at 'em!"
58 Argon or neon
59 Alias letters

DOWN

1 *Squawk Box* network
2 Quiz answer
3 Mineo et al.
4 Mulcahy, on *M*A*S*H*
5 Pi follower
6 Long story
7 *Popeye* kid
8 Huckleberry __ (toon)
9 Bobby of hockey
10 '30s film studio
11 Snaky letter
16 *The Patty Duke Show* family
20 *Person to Person* host
22 Greg Gumbel's brother
24 Intends
25 *Star __: Deep Space Nine*
26 Bugs Bunny features
27 Actress Ione
28 Nasty
29 Shade trees
31 The man from U.N.C.L.E., for one: Abbr.
34 *Upstairs, Downstairs* setting
35 Mrs. Phil Donahue
40 Norwegian playwright
42 Feels sore
44 Air pollution
46 Composer of Carson's theme
47 Smell bad
48 Actress Sedgwick
49 Baton Rouge school: Abbr.
50 "Alley __!"
51 Singing syllable
53 Florida neighbor: Abbr.

1	2	3		4	5	6		7	8	9	10	11
12				13				14				
15			16					17				
18						19	20					
			21		22		23			24	25	26
27	28	29			30	31				32		
33				34				35				
36				37				38				
39			40				41	42				
			43			44		45		46	47	48
49	50	51				52	53					
54						55				56		
57						58				59		

16 FRESH PRINCE OF BEL AIR

Bel Air Academy, Bel Air, California

ACROSS

1 Great, in rap-speak
5 *Lou Grant* newspaper
9 Garfield, for one
12 Cuss word
13 Cher's '60s partner
14 Hardwood tree
15 She portrayed a girlfriend of 51 Across
17 Mr. Romano
18 Pop singer __ Marie
19 Cry of pain
21 Compass point: Abbr.
22 Scale note
25 "Sing Along" guy
28 __ Flytrap (WKRP DJ)
30 Knucklehead
31 Jose Jimenez portrayer
34 Prefix for system
35 __ even keel
36 Norse god
37 Harry Hamlin legal series
39 Craig T. Nelson sitcom
41 Lawn material
42 Freddie the Freeloader, e.g.
45 Boxer Spinks
47 *Our Gang* girl
49 Styling gel, for instance
51 Star of the show
54 Sally Field, in a '60s sitcom
55 602, in Roman numerals
56 Real-estate unit
57 Porky __
58 Cry of pain
59 Close by

DOWN

1 *Designing Women* star
2 Shepherd's *Moonlighting* role
3 Up __ (stuck)
4 "Stronger __ dirt"
5 Schedule open-slot abbreviation
6 Director Howard
7 Deep black
8 __ *Buddies* (Tom Hanks sitcom)
9 51 Across' best friend
10 Hungry __ bear
11 "Love __ Neighbor"
16 Gomer Pyle's home
20 Lucy Carter, on *The Lucy Show*
23 First-year student, on *The Paper Chase*
24 __ *Tanner* (David Hartman series)
26 Tax expert: Abbr.
27 Barnyard animal
28 Ethel Mertz portrayer
29 Robert Vaughn TV role
31 One of the Dwarfs
32 Ruckus
33 She portrayed a girlfriend of 51 Across
38 Does some arithmetic
40 "It's __ Doody time!"
42 Streisand Oscar role
43 Prefix for violet
44 *Politically Incorrect* host
46 Amiable
48 To __ (unanimously)
49 Economic statistic: Abbr.
50 Chevalier's assent
52 __ *Abner*
53 Backtalk

1	2	3	4		5	6	7	8		9	10	11
12					13					14		
15				16						17		
18							19		20			
21				22	23	24		25			26	27
			28				29		30			
31	32	33			34				35			
36					37		38					
39				40		41				42	43	44
		45			46			47	48			
49	50			51		52	53					
54				55					56			
57				58					59			

17 FRIENDS

Greenwich Village, New York

ACROSS

1 Mach 2 planes
5 Like Oscar and Felix
8 Used to be
11 Flapjack chain's initials
12 Neither's partner
13 Meyers of *Kate & Allie*
14 Character on the show
17 Oscar and Felix's game
18 Steve Forrest action series of the '70s
19 *Cheers* character
21 Dave Garroway's signoff
25 *Tic __ Dough*
28 "That is all __!"
31 Granny portrayer on *The Beverly Hillbillies*
32 Inventor Whitney
33 Aniston's role on the show
35 Self-image
36 Hoss' older brother
38 Russell of *Felicity*
39 Method: Abbr.
40 Animal seen in *Northern Exposure*
42 VCR button
44 *You Bet Your Life*, for one
47 *Falcon Crest* character
51 Portrayer of 14 Across
54 Santa __, California
55 Numerical prefix
56 Marathon unit
57 Mr. Serling
58 "Alley __!"
59 Byrnes of *77 Sunset Strip* et al.

DOWN

1 Noodlebrain
2 "Get outta here!"
3 Honky-__ piano
4 Cosby and Culp, in the '60s
5 Off __ tangent
6 Frequent sitcom family pets
7 Actress Barrymore
8 Radar O'Reilly's real first name
9 "__ You Lonesome Tonight?"
10 What corporals call colonels
15 TV's Batgirl
16 Pool-race unit
20 Game-show producer Goodson
22 Affirmative votes
23 Shrewd
24 *Dukes of Hazzard* spinoff
25 Bad News Bears, for one
26 Actor __ Ray
27 Italian farewell
29 Look at
30 TV's Galloping Gourmet
34 Penny, to Sky King
37 '50s Lee Marvin police series
41 Corsica's continent: Abbr.
43 Binghamton's catchphrase on *McHale's Navy*
45 *Leave __ Beaver*
46 Nada
48 Acetic or nitric
49 Real-estate sign
50 Lou Grant and Edie, for example
51 *My Mother the __* ('60s sitcom)
52 Sean Lennon's mom
53 Small bite

The local hangout is the Central Perk coffeehouse.

Ross' (David Schwimmer's) pet monkey was Marcel.

The show's theme song: "I'll Be There for You," is performed by the Rembrandts.

18 GET SMART

CONTROL Headquarters, Washington, D.C.

ACROSS

1 *The Ghost and Mrs. __*
5 Huntley and Brinkley, e.g.
9 *Gunsmoke* network
12 Norway's capital
13 Taj Mahal city
14 Conjunction on *Concentration*
15 Co-creator of the show
17 Peeples or Long
18 Sounds of acknowledgment
19 *Hee Haw* cohost
21 Jay Silverheels TV role
24 "Who __ Turn To?"
26 One: Fr.
27 Barbie or Ken
29 Former Italian money
33 Agent 99 portrayer on the show
36 Ronny's TV dad
37 Hall of *Saturday Night Live*
38 Mork's home
39 *Star __: Deep Space Nine*
41 *The Man From U.N.C.L.E.* character
43 Part of VCR
46 Sault __ Marie
47 Generation
48 Co-creator of the show
54 "The Big Mooseketeer"
55 '60s secret-agent series
56 Menageries
57 Response: Abbr.
58 Sergeants, for example: Abbr.
59 GI's offense: Abbr.

DOWN

1 June Cleaver or Harriet Nelson
2 Find a job for
3 Under the weather
4 Hymie, on the show
5 Marshal McCloud's hometown
6 Swelled head
7 Biblical boat
8 Raymond Burr TV role
9 Shape of Beldar's head
10 *Diff'rent Strokes* star
11 Spanish ladies: Abbr.
16 Friend of Mary Richards
20 Geer of *The Waltons*
21 Marching-band instruments
22 __ upswing (rising)
23 Propeller head
24 *American Bandstand* host
25 __ Romeo
28 "Eat __ eaten"
30 David Cassidy, in the '70s
31 Western actor Calhoun
32 "Times of Your Life" singer
34 Computer storage unit
35 Gloria Stivic's mother
40 Burt Ward TV role
42 Celebrity interviewer Gibbons
43 *Alice* waitress
44 Smeltery metal
45 __ *of Our Lives* (soap opera)
46 "The __ the limit!"
49 Los Angeles school: Abbr.
50 __ *Sharkey* (Rickles sitcom)
51 At this moment
52 Down under jumper
53 Fashion monogram

The first name of the Chief (Edward Platt) was Thaddeus; his last name was never revealed.

Bernie Kopell portrayed KAOS villain Conrad Siegfried, before becoming the doctor on The Love Boat.

Hymie (Dick Gautier) weighed 982 pounds.

19 GILLIGAN'S ISLAND

Uncharted Desert Isle, South Pacific

ACROSS

1 *You Bet Your Life* host
5 Rerun month: Abbr.
8 Fruit drinks
12 Emeril, for one
13 Basic Cable channel
14 Room: Sp.
15 Wrecked ship in the show
17 "Terrible" kid's phase
18 Falsehood
19 Corbin Bernsen character
20 "Lonesome George" of '50s TV
23 Robin Hood weapon
25 Hazzard County deputy
26 Vending-machine opening
27 Always, in poetry
30 Run in
31 Tim Taylor's concern, on *Home Improvement*
32 Baton Rouge school: Abbr.
33 Call it a day
34 *Wiseguy* star
35 Pleased
36 Soaps actress Slezak
38 The Jetsons' robot
39 Jay's late-night follower
41 Hiatus
42 Letter holders: Abbr.
43 The Skipper portrayer on the show
48 *One __ Beyond* (sci-fi series)
49 *My Three Sons* grandpa
50 Mrs. Ernie Kovacs
51 British conservative
52 Poker card
53 Acting job

DOWN

1 Game-show hosts: Abbr.
2 Sounds of contentment
3 Sleep-stage letters
4 Scully and Mulder's concerns
5 Mrs. Ward Cleaver
6 GI hangout
7 Perry Mason's expertise
8 The Jetsons' dog
9 Mary Ann portrayer on the show
10 *The Time Machine* race
11 Return-postage courtesy: Abbr.
16 Zero
19 Painting and sculpture
20 Rayburn of *The Match Game*
21 __ even keel
22 Gilligan portrayer on the show
23 Magnum's farewell
24 "Shake, Rattle and __"
26 Drench
28 Morales of *NYPD Blue*
29 Ill-mannered
31 Mary Kate, to Ashley
35 *Love Boat* character
37 Like Selma Diamond's voice
38 Tried to get elected
39 "__ la vie!"
40 Not fooled by
41 Mr. Kotter
43 Lawyers' organization: Abbr.
44 Captain Jean-__ Picard
45 Fuss
46 Tiny, in Dogpatch
47 Shoebox letters

Lovey Howell's (Natalie Schafer's) perfume was Gold Dust No. 5.

The Skipper's (43 Across') real name was Jonas Grumby.

Thurston Howell III's (Jim Backus') nickname was "The Wolf of Wall Street."

20 THE GOLDEN GIRLS

6151 Richmond Street, Miami Beach, Florida

ACROSS

1 *Tracey Takes On . . .* network
4 Exercise discipline
8 Thread cluster
12 Furniture wood
13 Venus de Milo's lack
14 Eskimo dwelling
15 Mr. Wizard's specialty: Abbr.
16 A star of the show
18 Michigan J. Frog's network
20 *Father Murphy* star
21 Solo of *Star Wars*
23 Overwhelm
24 TV clown
27 Captain Kirk's home state
29 *Mork & Mindy* network
32 A star of the show
35 Gobbled up
36 MGM film sound effect
37 Telejournalist Paula
38 *Dynasty* commodity
39 Peter Marshall's actress sister
41 *Hogan's Heroes* star

44 Emulate John Glenn
48 32 Across' role on the show
52 Oklahoma city
53 Director Kazan
54 Aaron Spelling's daughter
55 Reviewer Reed
56 Beer head
57 "I cannot tell __!"
58 Skater Babilonia

DOWN

1 Mr. Roarke, on *Fantasy Island*
2 Daisy Duke portrayer
3 *Grapes of Wrath* migrant
4 Start of a Fred Flintstone cheer
5 Source of metals
6 Morning show's initials
7 Quick __ wink
8 Duke or earl
9 Sounds of discomfort
10 Chimney passage
11 Go left or right
17 Dick Martin's partner

19 Interrogative pronoun
22 Actor Williamson
23 Emmy, for one
24 Bathing-suit part
25 No longer fashionable
26 Last letter
28 Slangy suffix
29 "I understand now!"
30 Scrooge exclamation
31 Aaron Brown's network
33 Colonial newsman
34 Côte d'__
38 A wee hour
40 Roker of *The Jeffersons*
41 G preceders
42 Transferred worker's benefit, for short
43 Nike competitor
45 One of Mrs. Krabappel's students
46 Notion
47 Judd Hirsch sitcom
49 Airline-screen stat: Abbr.
50 Owner of 31 Down
51 Mentalist Geller

21 GREEN ACRES

Hooterville, U.S.A.

ACROSS

1 Office seeker, for short
4 Elly __ Clampett
7 Dobie Gillis' pursuer
12 Alias: Abbr.
13 __ Jima
14 *Peyton Place* star
15 Pat Buttram's role on the show
17 Actress Witherspoon
18 Carter, to Gomer Pyle
19 "__ the fields we go . . ."
21 Botch
23 Sitcom producer Lear
28 Alphabetic trio
31 Null and __
33 Skier's gear
34 With 54 Across, Gabor and Albert's roles on the show
37 Aide: Abbr.
38 *The Naked Truth* character
39 Environment-friendly prefix
40 Guinan portrayer on *Star Trek: The Next Generation*
42 Shoemaker's tool
44 Very wide, as a shoe
46 *60 Minutes* reporter
50 Olsen of *The Brady Bunch*
54 See 34 Across
56 Patty Duke ex
57 "__ never heard them at all, till there was you"
58 Columnist Kupcinet
59 Dylan McKay on *Beverly Hills 90210*
60 Rental dwelling: Abbr.
61 Cookbook abbreviation

DOWN

1 Dawber's namesakes
2 Cajun vegetable
3 Cowardly Lion portrayer
4 Urecal of *The Adventures of Tugboat Annie*
5 Stupefy
6 Tom Smothers hobby
7 Guy Williams TV role
8 Compass point: Abbr.
9 Michele of *Knots Landing*
10 Hamilton Burger et al.: Abbr.
11 Dark brew
16 Mature
20 *Bewitched* character
22 Schell of *Gomer Pyle, U.S.M.C.*
24 New York engineering school: Abbr.
25 Relocate
26 Actor Baldwin
27 Fictional sleuth __ Wolfe
28 Eagle's gripper
29 Plate
30 Exxon's former name
32 Wedding vow
35 From __ Z
36 Mackenzie Brackman case
41 *Lost in Space* character
43 Fall behind
45 *Laverne & Shirley* character
47 Scurry about
48 Jug handles
49 Reply to an invitation
50 Patsy
51 Take off the shelf
52 Orchestra section: Abbr.
53 Broadcast
55 "Alley __!"

34 Across' cow was named Eleanor.

34 Across' farm was 160 acres.

15 Across' first name was Eustace.

22 HAPPY DAYS

565 North Clinton Drive, Milwaukee, Wisconsin

ACROSS

1 1400, in Roman numerals
4 __ Mr. Wizard
7 *That Girl* name
12 Cry of discovery
13 New Deal agency: Abbr.
14 Butter substitutes
15 Catchphrase of 55 Across on the show
17 Donny Most's role on the show
18 Reach across
19 Visitors from space: Abbr.
21 Rah relative
22 Blonde shade
25 Magazine publisher, familiarly
27 Eisenhower's monogram
30 Thompson of *Family*
32 Road Runner's sound
36 Potsie Weber portrayer on the show
39 Bea Arthur's husband on *Maude*
40 In the center of
41 Victor Buono's *Batman* role
42 Waikiki souvenir
44 __ *Baba and the 40 Thieves*
46 Urban mail center: Abbr.
49 Ignited
51 Half of a Mork farewell
55 With 57 Across, Fonzie portrayer on the show
57 See 55 Across
60 Gossip-column paragraphs
61 Wedding phrase
62 *The __ Valley* (Stanwyck series)
63 *Dukes of Hazzard* uncle
64 Slangy turndown
65 Beer relative

DOWN

1 Connecticut neighbor
2 *My Three Sons* kid
3 Captain Picard's android officer
4 *One Day at a Time* mom
5 Lanka
6 Jackson of *Charlie's Angels*
7 David Janssen's TV pursuer
8 Pie __ mode
9 Depend (on)
10 Run easily
11 Job-safety agency: Abbr.
16 "Put __ Happy Face"
20 Tuesday Weld's *Dobie Gillis* role
23 Job ID, often: Abbr.
24 Magnum's home
26 *The __* (Zimbalist, Jr. series)
27 Beaver's creation
28 Double-helix molecule
29 Computer-keyboard key
31 __ sum (Chinese appetizer)
33 Have a snack
34 Australian bird
35 Hollywood clock setting: Abbr.
37 Popeye's love
38 The "bad" cholesterol: Abbr.
43 Alex P. Keaton's mom
45 Pen filler
46 Alphabetic quartet
47 __ *and Gladys* ('60s sitcom)
48 Change for a five
50 Exact match
52 Jessica of *Dark Angel*
53 *Topper* dog
54 Press for
56 Hotel accommodations: Abbr.
58 Nancy Walker's *Rhoda* role
59 Right away

Potsie Weber's real first name on the show was Warren.

Fonzie's real first name was Arthur.

The local lovers' lane was Inspiration Point.

23 THE HONEYMOONERS

Chauncey Street, Brooklyn, New York

ACROSS

1 Social slight
5 Sergeant Friday
8 Ones in charge: Abbr.
12 South American country
13 Sounds of delight
14 Very wide shoe
15 A star of the show
18 Checkbook parts
19 *Nanny and the Professor* star
20 Beast of burden
22 *Masterpiece Theatre* source
23 Jagger of *Mr. Novak*
26 Canine wagger
28 In addition
31 A star of the show
34 __ Ann Nivens (*Mary Tyler Moore Show* character)
35 Offend the nose
36 *Seinfeld* "etc."
37 G-man
38 Where Mork came from
40 Arbus of *M*A*S*H*
43 *That Was the Week That Was* host
47 A star of the show
51 Assist in a crime
52 *The Waltons* store owner
53 Two semesters
54 Ron Howard's *Happy Days* mom
55 Julia Sweeney *SNL* character
56 Major-__ (butler)

DOWN

1 Health resorts
2 Like "it": Abbr.
3 Language of Pakistan
4 Home of NBC's California studios
5 Late-night TV name
6 Electrical unit
7 Language suffix
8 Richard Boone series before *Have Gun Will Travel*
9 Rock science: Abbr.
10 Whimper
11 *Touched by an Angel* character
16 Curved letter
17 Walk slowly
21 Emma Peel associate
22 Phil Silvers character
23 WKRP employees: Abbr.
24 __ de Cologne
25 Onetime Cable TV award
27 Improve, as wine
28 Hungry __ bear
29 Silent assent
30 High-tech "fingerprint"
32 Ryan of *The Beverly Hillbillies*
33 Cohort of Radner and Curtin
37 Sergeant Friday's quest
39 *Mayberry, __*
40 Slightly open
41 Claude Akins TV role
42 Soap ingredients
44 Vegetable-based spread
45 Unwanted e-mail
46 "Comin' __ the Rye"
48 Taylor of *The $1.98 Beauty Show*
49 Pseudonym letters
50 Tennis need

31 Across' employer was the Gotham Bus Company.

The instrumental theme, "You're My Greatest Love," was written by 31 Across.

The local Chinese restaurant was Hong Kong Gardens.

24 I DREAM OF JEANNIE

1020 Palm Drive, Cocoa Beach, Florida

ACROSS

1 Backus and Henson
5 Mire
9 Teachers' union: Abbr.
12 __ 12 ('70s police series)
13 Like __ of bricks
14 Where Mork and Mindy honeymooned
15 Downey of *Touched by an Angel*
16 Princess of India
17 By way of
18 A star of the show
21 One __ customer
22 Stanley Cup organization: Abbr.
23 Corporate execs: Abbr.
26 Cellular material
28 Jon Provost's *Lassie* role
32 *Star Trek: The Next Generation* character
34 Nothing
36 *Miami __* (Don Johnson series)
37 Dick Van Dyke's role in *Diagnosis Murder*
39 Door buster

41 Rummy variety
42 Modern music style
44 __ long way (last)
46 A star of the show
51 The Batmobile, e.g.
52 Small bills
53 Joe Isuzu, memorably
55 Porky or Petunia
56 Cincinnati baseballers
57 Not __ many words
58 *Hollywood Squares* win
59 Plumlike fruit
60 Use the transporter

DOWN

1 Peanut-butter container
2 Fan club's focus
3 __'s *Family* (Vicki Lawrence sitcom)
4 Agent 86
5 *Gilligan's Island* character
6 Home of the Osmonds
7 Late-night TV name
8 Ted Baxter portrayer
9 PBS science show
10 Moran of *Joanie Loves Chachi*

11 Alias: Abbr.
19 *Night Gallery* name
20 1054, in Roman numerals
23 Microbuses and Beetles: Abbr.
24 Vote seeker
25 Hit-show sign
27 Atmosphere
29 Russian fighter plane
30 Sprint competitor
31 Longing
33 Corporal Klinger portrayer
35 Food Network chef
38 Gomer Pyle portrayer
40 *Simpsons* tavern owner
43 *To Tell the Truth* group
45 *Whose Line Is It Anyway?* stock-in-trade
46 Scott of *Joanie Loves Chachi*
47 Golden Fleece ship
48 Make over
49 __ *kleine Nachtmusik*
50 Employer of 18 Across on the show: Abbr.
51 Naval noncom: Abbr.
54 CD-__

46 Across' invisible dog was Djinn Djinn.

1
2
3
4
5
6
7
8
9
10
11
12
13
14
15
16
17
18
19
20
21
22
23
24
25
26
27
28
29
30
31
32
33
34
35
36
37
38
39
40
41
42
43
44
45
46
47
48
49
50
51
52
53
54
55
56
57
58
59
60

Farrah Fawcett appeared during the show's last season, as Roger Healy's (Bill Daily's) girlfriend.

The producer of the show was author Sidney Sheldon.

25 I LOVE LUCY

623 East 68th Street, New York, New York

ACROSS

1 Morrow of *Northern Exposure*
4 Family member
7 Sheep's sound
12 __ out a living
13 Chapter of history
14 Type of short-answer question
15 Fred Mertz portrayer on the show
17 *3rd Rock From the Sun* network
18 Gilbert of *Roseanne*
19 Military offense: Abbr.
21 Jaffe of *Ben Casey*
24 Tonys and Emmys
28 Nautical direction
31 *The Avengers* star
33 Director Ephron
34 Where 53 Across works on the show
37 Former *Entertainment Tonight* host
38 Swiss abstract painter
39 Flightless bird
40 Street where Bert and Ernie live
42 Train lines: Abbr.
44 Simon __ (kids' game)
46 Johnny Carson predecessor
50 Colleague of Wallace and Bradley
53 Desi Arnaz's role on the show
56 Where ships dock
57 Afternoon hour
58 Greek letter
59 __ *Prince of Bel Air*
60 Media conglomerate initials
61 Paramedic: Abbr.

DOWN

1 Basketball officials
2 Gumbo ingredient
3 Gentle Ben, for one
4 *The Dick Van Dyke Show* character
5 Mine rock
6 Poet Angelou
7 "He should have been home __!"
8 Joey Tribbiani on *Friends*
9 Computer keyboard key
10 Industrious insect
11 "Mazel __!"
16 Used to be
20 *Hart to Hart* star
22 Nickname of Onassis
23 Most popular Disney toon
25 Something to cast
26 Instrument for 53 Across
27 Actor from India
28 *Law & Order* characters: Abbr.
29 On the house
30 Easy throw
32 Guy's date
35 *Star Trek* weapons
36 Prefix meaning "atmosphere"
41 *Upstairs, Downstairs* star
43 Health resort
45 Spanish miss: Abbr.
47 Johnson of *Laugh-In*
48 West of *Batman*
49 Runaway victory
50 Letters on a sunblock bottle
51 On the __ (broadcasting)
52 Service charge
54 __ Jima
55 General's subordinate: Abbr.

Lucy's maiden name on the show was MacGillicuddy.

The Mertzes' pet dog was Butch.

53 Across' name in the pilot episode was Larry Lopez.

26 THE JEFFERSONS

Deluxe Apartment in the Sky, New York, New York

ACROSS

1 Mr. T's '80s TV group
6 Charlie Rose's network
9 Thermometer unit: Abbr.
12 *Wheel of Fortune* name
13 Acorn source
14 Have another birthday
15 John Forsythe, on *Bachelor Father*
16 With 45 Across, a star of the show
18 Fall month: Abbr.
20 Onetime *Hollywood Squares* regular
21 *Fantasy Island* character
25 Had a snack
26 Danny DeVito's wife
27 *The Godfather* author
29 The Lakers' league: Abbr.
32 A star of the show
35 *Charlie's Angels* nickname
36 Crystal-ball user
37 Phrase used by a 36 Across
38 Farm enclosure
39 Neophyte doctor
41 Ms. Couric
44 Skater Babilonia
45 See 16 Across
47 First name of Florence's portrayer on the show
52 Live and breathe
53 Sportscaster Berman
54 Hoops star Shaquille
55 "Smoking or __?"
56 Supplement, with "out"
57 "__ dabba doo!"

DOWN

1 Slugger's stat: Abbr.
2 Driveway material
3 Compass point: Abbr.
4 Director __ Lee
5 Toon voiced by Jim Backus
6 Alan Young, on *Mister Ed*
7 Ebenezer exclamation
8 Freddie the Freeloader portrayer
9 Rhett Butler's last word
10 Old-style oath
11 TV reviewer Shalit
17 Sandwich bread
19 Teri of *We Got It Made*
21 Lou Grant's paper
22 Remark of recognition
23 Darjeeling and pekoe
24 Actor Hunter
25 Hank of *The Simpsons*
28 Take off the shelf
29 Have a __ for news
30 __ Rabbit (Joel Chandler Harris character)
31 Mideast gulf
33 Getty of *The Golden Girls*
34 In good shape
38 Family member
40 Mr. Spock portrayer
41 Genghis __
42 Prefix for nautical
43 Federal agents
44 Daly of *Judging Amy*
46 "A mouse!"
48 Santa __, California
49 Civil War soldier
50 Experimentation room
51 Pie __ mode

27 LAVERNE & SHIRLEY

730 Knapp Street, Milwaukee, Wisconsin

ACROSS

1 Alphabetic trio
4 Nonfielding baseball positions: Abbr.
7 Davis of *Evening Shade*
12 Australian bird
13 Talent for music
14 Javelin
15 Shirley portrayer
18 C.P.O. Sharkey's first name
19 Charged atom
20 *Falcon __*
24 "There oughta be __!"
28 Emulate Picabo Street
31 *__ in the Family*
32 *Battlestar Galactica* genre
33 Laverne portrayer
36 Bob Barker or Tom Bergeron
37 Feline, to Tweety
38 Scotch alternative
39 "__ I say, not . . ."
40 *Touched by an Angel* star
42 Compass point: Abbr.
44 Will of *The Waltons*
48 Eddie Mekka's role on the show
54 *I Love Lucy* star
55 Super Bowl organizer: Abbr.
56 Tachometer reading: Abbr.
57 Telejournalist Sawyer
58 Dentist's degree: Abbr.
59 Light-switch positions

DOWN

1 Art __
2 Give off
3 *Candid Camera* creator
4 Laurie Partridge portrayer
5 *Hee __*
6 __ Lanka
7 Capital of Norway
8 Popeye's power source
9 Caribbean, for example
10 "__ a Rock" (Paul Simon tune)
11 Sounds of hesitation
16 Welby or Kildare
17 Ignited
21 Comic Martha
22 Peyton Place's main street
23 Fred Flintstone's boss
25 Falsehood teller
26 "He wouldn't hurt __!"
27 __ E. Coyote
28 Exceeded the limit
29 __ Sabe
30 Ancient South American
32 Some Air France jets
34 WKRP employee
35 Charlotte of *The Facts of Life*
40 Toon Chihuahua
41 Silly Putty holder
43 42 extra long or 12EEE
45 Parisian's new money
46 Fox Sports Channel rival
47 Door breakers
48 Rogue
49 Bush press secretary Fleischer
50 Single-strand molecule
51 Football position
52 *Mayberry __*
53 Roker's namesakes

15 Across' stuffed cat was Boo-Boo Kitty.

The local hangout was the Pizza Bowl.

33 Across' favorite drink was Pepsi and milk.

28 LEAVE IT TO BEAVER

211 Pine Street, Mayfield, U.S.A.

ACROSS

1 __ Albert (Cosby character)
4 Stapleton of *All in the Family*
8 __ Na Na
11 Actress Thurman
12 Ye __ Tea Shoppe
13 Clothing border
14 Beaver Cleaver portrayer
17 Bartender on *The Love Boat*
18 Agricultural tool
19 Didn't sell
22 Napoleon Solo's employer
26 *The A-Team* character
29 Dan Blocker TV role
31 Point at the target
32 Shoemaker's hole puncher
33 Wally Cleaver's wise-guy pal
34 Sunshine State school: Abbr.
35 Cohort of Shemp and Larry
36 Wise __ owl
37 Mediterranean and Caribbean

38 Bugs Bunny's pursuer
40 Dick of *Bewitched*
42 Call __ day (turn in)
44 Sounds from a sty
48 Ward Cleaver portrayer
52 Fireplace residue
53 David Frost, for one
54 Antique auto
55 Soaked
56 Ivy League school
57 Kitten sound

DOWN

1 *McHale's Navy* character
2 Mingo portrayer on *Daniel Boone*
3 Linda Thorson, on *The Avengers*
4 TV psychologist Brothers
5 Shade tree
6 City in Oklahoma
7 Where Amsterdam is: Abbr.
8 *The West Wing* star
9 That woman
10 Mornings: Abbr.
15 Garden tool

16 *Full __* (Saget sitcom)
20 Professors' degrees: Abbr.
21 *Good Morning America* rival
23 __ Nervosa (*Frasier* hangout)
24 Loring of *The Addams Family*
25 Australian birds
26 __ and fortune
27 GI offense: Abbr.
28 Red Skelton character
30 Prefix meaning "Chinese"
33 *Lost in Space* launch point
37 Read quickly
39 Prime-time hour
41 __ 66 (Milner/Maharis series)
43 Actress Dalton
45 George Wendt TV role
46 Leg joint
47 Store away
48 *Hee __*
49 Take advantage of
50 Pitcher's stat: Abbr.
51 Be sick

The exterior of the Cleaver home was used again for Marcus Welby, M.D.

The show's instrumental theme was "The Toy Parade."

June Cleaver's (Barbara Billingsley's) maiden name was Bronson.

29 MAD ABOUT YOU

51 Fifth Avenue, New York, New York

ACROSS

1 *Entertainment Tonight* cohost
5 Unkempt one
9 Taylor or Serling
12 ". . . __ saw Elba"
13 Baba __ (Radner character)
14 *Three __ Match* (Bill Cullen game show)
15 Paul Buchman's occupation on the show
17 Missouri city: Abbr.
18 *The A-Team* star
19 Opinion piece
21 *Roots* won nine of them
24 *M*A*S*H* nickname
26 One of the Dwarfs
27 African language
28 Paul Buchman's work specialty on the show
34 Gomez Addams' favorite dance
35 Vaccine target
36 Doris of *Everybody Loves Raymond*
39 *Dukes of Hazzard* uncle
41 Pile up
42 Gotham City crime-fighting symbol
43 German article
44 A star of the show
50 Farm industry: Abbr.
51 Maturing agent
52 Actor Morales
53 Walston of *My Favorite Martian*
54 Richard of *The Big Valley*
55 Conan O'Brien preceder

DOWN

1 Magazine publisher's nickname
2 *Exodus* character
3 Family member: Abbr.
4 Lassie's '50s master
5 '70s Steve Forrest series
6 "Mighty __ a Rose"
7 Be obligated to
8 Robert Blake TV role
9 *Peyton Place* doctor
10 Available
11 Actress Tyne's family
16 *The Ghost and __ Muir*
20 Speak unclearly
21 55 Across announcer Hall
22 Bovine sound
23 1200, in old Rome
24 Puts up a picture
25 Not fooled by
27 Crooked
29 Western Indians
30 McCloud's title
31 "No __, ands, or buts!"
32 Overhead trains
33 __ Ellen (*Dallas* character)
36 Walter O'Reilly's nickname
37 Last Greek letter
38 First host of *The Joker's Wild*
39 One of the Brady kids
40 *I Love Lucy* character
42 Gertrude of early sitcoms
45 Conceit
46 Author Deighton
47 Put to work
48 One of the Bobbsey Twins
49 Uncle, in Mexico

The family dog was Murray.

The local watering hole was Riff's Bar.

44 Across' parents were portrayed by Carol Burnett and Carroll O'Connor.

30 THE MANY LOVES OF DOBIE GILLIS

285 Norwood Street, Central City, U.S.A.

ACROSS

1 Days: Sp.
5 Source of syrup
8 Western writer Grey
12 *My Friend* __ ('50s sitcom)
13 __ *Day at a Time*
14 Person in debt
15 Bob Denver's role on the show
18 Three, in Germany
19 Richard Roeper's partner
20 With 37 Across, Milton Armitage portrayer on the show
23 Peeples of *Fame*
24 Two-dimensional extent
25 Corporate bigwig's plane
26 WWII president
29 *Kidnapped* author's monogram
30 *Hazel* star
32 Bud's partner
33 On the __ (precisely)
34 Actress __ Dawn Chong
35 Hazel's occupation
36 __ *for Evidence* (Grafton novel)
37 See 20 Across
39 Rhea Perlman TV role
42 Bachelor of __
43 Star of the show
48 Hawaiian neckwear
49 Fishing gear
50 Roof overhang
51 Not working
52 Roll-call vote
53 Made a sketch

DOWN

1 Poorly lit
2 *Mad About You* cousin
3 Actress Brenneman
4 Milton Berle's mother
5 Tabitha of MTV
6 *The King* __
7 *Married . . . With Children* character
8 Ben Casey's mentor
9 Bide-__
10 Where Omaha is: Abbr.
11 Prefix for while
16 Live and breathe
17 See 30 Down
20 Burt of *Batman*
21 Singer Guthrie
22 Shady __ (*Petticoat Junction* hotel)
23 Aerialist's protection
25 Mannix's first name
26 Like a prairie
27 __-yourself kit
28 *The Cosby Show* girl
30 With 17 Down, *Family Affair* star
31 Western Hemisphere alliance: Abbr.
35 Like the Lone Ranger
36 Alex P. Keaton's mom
37 *December* __ (Spring Byington sitcom)
38 And so on: Abbr.
39 451, in Roman numerals
40 Very impressed
41 Banister
42 Nautical greeting
44 The Big Band __
45 Scratch up
46 Street crosser: Abbr.
47 Freshly made

31 MARRIED . . . WITH CHILDREN

Jeopardy Lane, Chicago, Illinois

ACROSS

1 Beery of
   The Rockford Files
5 Draft organization:
   Abbr.
8 William Shatner TV
   role
12 Author Ferber
13 Airline bought by
   American
14 Bank need
15 *Friends* friend
   Chandler __
16 Wife/mother on the
   show
18 *Concentration* puzzle
20 __ de Cologne
21 Johnny of
   21 Jump Street
23 Portrayer of 16 Across
28 Neat __ pin
30 Alphabetic sequence
33 "Name That __"
34 Bud portrayer on the
   show
37 Footnote abbreviation
38 *Newsweek* rival
39 __ Angeles
40 Quincy Jones
   specialty

42 British noble
44 Shakespearean witch
47 Emulate Gabe Kotter
50 Al portrayer on the
   show
55 Hindu instructor
56 Electronics company
57 Ms. McClanahan
58 Radio deejay Don
59 Sampras of tennis
60 Watch on TV
61 Hide and __

DOWN

1 Midwest state:
   Abbr.
2 *Garfield* dog
3 Alice on
   The Brady Bunch
4 Albert of *Fame*
5 "The racer's edge"
6 __'Pea (*Popeye* infant)
7 *The Forsyte* __
8 School at Frankfort:
   Abbr.
9 Ziering of
   Beverly Hills 90210
10 Post-office
   abbreviation
11 Door opener

17 Kramden drove one
19 Accelerated
22 Fizzling sound
24 Arnie Becker, for one:
   Abbr.
25 *Benson* star
26 Part of A.D.
27 Most with August
   birthdays
28 Take __ view of
29 *Elephant Boy* actor
31 Moo goo __ pan
32 Actor Cronyn
35 Former dictator Amin
36 Bench or couch
41 Friend of Fidel
43 Kelly's talk partner
45 Broadcasts
46 Substance on stamps
48 Mötley __ (rock
   group)
49 Corn covering
50 Uncommon sense:
   Abbr.
51 Forest female
52 Where Toronto is:
   Abbr.
53 Louis of *The Beverly
   Hillbillies*
54 Majors or Marvin

Al (50 Across) worked at Gary's Shoe Emporium.

16 Across' maiden name was Wanker.

The family dog was Buck.

32 THE MARY TYLER MOORE SHOW

119 North Weatherly Avenue, Minneapolis, Minnesota

ACROSS

1 *The Seven Year __*
5 *Hill Street Blues* characters
9 Dr. Frankenstein's workplace
12 City in Alaska
13 Song for two
14 Poetic preposition
15 53 Across' wife on the show
17 Mobile's state: Abbr.
18 27 Down portrayer on the show
19 *The Mary Tyler Moore Show*, for one
21 Installs a lawn
24 Slangy refusal
25 Harris of *thirtysomething*
28 Sail the seven __
30 Naval rank: Abbr.
33 The Dynamic __ (Batman and Robin)
34 Allen Funt's order
36 Exist
37 Brandon of *The Courtship of Eddie's Father*
39 Nose-in-the-air type
40 *Friends* setting
41 Republicans: Abbr.
43 Challenge for the Sweathogs
45 Storch/Tucker series
48 *All My Children* character
52 "Gotcha!"
53 WJM anchorman on the show
56 Do a marathon
57 Captain Picard's counselor
58 Boxing match
59 B.A. Baracus portrayer
60 Agenda, for short
61 Writer Bombeck

DOWN

1 Swenson of *Benson*
2 Sock inserts
3 Slangy encouraging word
4 "__ Johnny!"
5 Letters after B
6 No longer fashionable
7 Dogs and cats
8 *Win Ben __'s Money*
9 Phyllis Lindstrom portrayer on the show
10 Singer Guthrie
11 Use the transporter
16 Michael of *Family Ties*
20 Tic-__-toe
22 41 Across rivals: Abbr.
23 Roger Moore TV role
25 1600, in Roman numerals
26 Where Iberia is: Abbr.
27 Boss on the show
29 __ gin fizz
31 Arid
32 Button on a VCR
35 *Barnaby Jones* star
38 San Diego attraction
42 Annie of *Designing Women*
44 The Hekawis, for instance
45 *Green Acres* setting
46 Calendar abbrevation
47 Central __ (*Friends* hangout)
49 Composer Stravinsky
50 Good buddy
51 "__ boy!"
54 Female deer
55 Josh around

Rhoda Morgenstern (Valerie Harper) worked at Hempel's department store.

53 Across' signoff line was "Good night and good news."

The show's theme song was "Love Is All Around."

33

M*A*S*H

Uijongbu, South Korea

ACROSS

1 Right-angle shape
4 Eye-bending designs
9 Trapper John, to 15 Across
12 Company bigwig: Abbr.
13 Antic
14 Vigoda of *Fish*
15 Alan Alda's role on the show
18 *Peyton Place* star
19 *Hollywood Squares* non-winner
20 Frog relative
23 Not at all capable
27 First name of Houlihan's portrayer on the show
30 Lauder of cosmetics
31 *People __ Funny* (Linkletter show)
32 Alphabetic trio
34 Brother or sister: Abbr.
35 Ewing family home
38 B.J. portrayer on the show
41 Shortened conjunction
42 Place to learn CPR
43 Shade tree
45 $100 bill
49 Harry Morgan's role on the show
54 Bodybuilder's muscles
55 Actor Flynn
56 Pig __ poke
57 Spinning toy
58 La __ (Italian opera house)
59 Boulevard relatives: Abbr.

DOWN

1 Reverberate
2 Not fatty
3 Seaborn portrayer on *The West Wing*
4 Honey West's Bruce
5 Fork over
6 Gorilla
7 Taken-back auto
8 Mrs. Ed Norton
9 Golf goal
10 *Happy Days* network
11 Actor Horsley
16 Jackson of *Charlie's Angels*
17 Very long time
21 Had a bite
22 Bugs Bunny colleague
24 Raison d'__
25 *The Avengers* character
26 *To __ the Truth*
27 Actress __ Flynn Boyle
28 Kind of vaccine
29 Monthly payment
33 Leg, slangily
36 *The Sonny and __ Comedy Hour*
37 *Dawson's Creek* star
39 Pepsi competitor
40 Talk wildly
44 __ Antony
46 *The Andy Griffith Show* character
47 Circus structure
48 Generations
49 Took a load off
50 *Arli$$* network
51 Mentalist's claim: Abbr.
52 New Deal agency: Abbr.
53 Officeholder, for short

49 Across' horse was Sophie.

1	2	3	■	4	5	6	7	8	■	9	10	11
12			■	13					■	14		
15			16					■	17			
18					■		19			■	■	■
■	■	■	20		21	22	■	23		24	25	26
27	28	29					■	30				
31			■	32		33		■	34			
35			36	37	■	38		39	40			
41					■	42				■	■	■
■	■	■	43		44	■	■	45		46	47	48
49	50	51			■	52	53					
54			■	55				■	■	56		
57			■	58				■	■	59		

Radar's (Gary Burghoff's) hometown was Ottumwa, Iowa.

His pet rabbits were Fluffy and Bongo.

34 MCHALE'S NAVY

Taratupa Island, South Pacific

ACROSS

1 Egyptian king
4 Pinball infraction
8 Olivia of *The Wonder Years*
12 "Now I understand!"
13 Air-freshener target
14 Banking devices: Abbr.
15 Star of the show
17 Dan Rather's specialty
18 *Just __ Me* (George Segal sitcom)
19 Stan of jazz
21 Swampy ground
23 Shirley Booth sitcom
27 *__ Goes On* (Patti LuPone series)
30 Merit
33 Keogh relative
34 54 Across' nickname
37 151, in old Rome
38 *The X-Files* investigations
39 Ascend
40 *The Odd Couple* character
42 Greek letter
44 *Let's Make a Deal* choice
47 Willie of *Eight Is Enough*
51 Ricky Ricardo portrayer
54 Captain Binghamton portrayer on the show
56 *Leave __ Beaver*
57 Suit to __
58 ". . . __ thousand times no!"
59 __ *of Our Lives*
60 Champagne bucket
61 Poisonous snake

DOWN

1 Typewriter settings
2 Cry of dread
3 Poi source
4 Jay Silverheels TV role
5 __ Amin
6 Richard of *Nanny and the Professor*
7 Oak or apple
8 *Family Law* star
9 Had brunch
10 Imported auto
11 CIA's forerunner
16 '60s *Hollywood Squares* regular
20 *The Cosby Show* kid
22 Steffi of tennis
24 Tubular pasta
25 Greek love god
26 Like some excuses
27 Plumb __
28 Misfortunes
29 Bank insurance agency: Abbr.
31 Fuss
32 Recipe abbreviation
35 France's new money
36 Frequent *L.A. Law* venue
41 Lone Ranger's farewell
43 *60 Minutes* reporter
45 Six Million Dollar Man's hometown
46 College military group: Abbr.
48 Talking bird
49 *The Dukes of Hazzard* spinoff
50 Break suddenly
51 Performed
52 Airport-screen stat.
53 Place for pigs
55 Wide shoe

McHale's first name on the show was Quinton.

The ship commanded by McHale was PT 73.

The setting of the final year of the show was the Italian town of Voltafiore.

1	2	3		4	5	6	7		8	9	10	11
12				13					14			
15			16						17			
18						19		20				
			21		22			23		24	25	26
27	28	29			30	31	32			33		
34				35					36			
37				38					39			
40			41				42	43				
			44		45	46		47		48	49	50
51	52	53			54		55					
56					57					58		
59					60					61		

35 MISTER ED

17230 Valley Spring Lane, Los Angeles, California

ACROSS

1 Ad __ (talk without a script)
4 Hugh O'Brian TV role
8 CNN talk host
12 *Wheel of Fortune* purchase
13 Not guilty, for example
14 College sports organization: Abbr.
15 *Alice* character
16 Star of the show
18 Boats of refuge
20 __ *the Press* (Sunday interview show)
21 Moe or Curly
24 TV dog star
28 P preceders
30 *Newhart* setting
31 What the title character is "always on," according to the theme song
37 Spelling contest
38 Author Anita
39 Michael J. Fox's homeland
43 *Mission: Impossible* leader
47 Peddle
49 Saddle or sofa
50 Voice of the title character
55 *Ben-__* (Heston film)
56 Lotion ingredient
57 Author Wiesel
58 Actress MacGraw
59 Fuse metal
60 Knock sharply

DOWN

1 Lorenzo of *Falcon Crest*
2 Not moving
3 Phil Silvers TV role
4 Clean-air agency: Abbr.
5 __ *in the Family*
6 Package of paper
7 *What's My Line?* quartet
8 __ *Landing* (*Dallas* spinoff)
9 Hospital area: Abbr.
10 One of the Bobbseys
11 One-liner
17 Affirmative vote
19 Seafood serving
22 A.M. show, for short
23 Cease
25 Title for a knight
26 __ and outs
27 Compass point: Abbr.
29 Olive of comics
31 22 Down's network
32 *Voyage to the Bottom of the __*
33 Prime-time hour
34 Crockett or Tubbs
35 __ and aah
36 Makes the most of
40 Gave a *Jeopardy!* response
41 *The Partridge Family* star
42 First *Tonight Show* host
44 Operetta composer Franz
45 TV reporter Zahn
46 *77 Sunset __*
48 Composer Schifrin
50 Uncooked
51 Grand __ Opry
52 Klink's rank: Abbr.
53 Small bite
54 Shoebox letters

The title character's lips were made to move by putting peanut butter in his mouth.

The real name of the horse was Bamboo Harvester.

50 Across had been a cowboy film star of the 1930s.

1	2	3	■	4	5	6	7	■	8	9	10	11
12			■	13				■	14			
15			■	16			■	17				
18			19			20				■	■	■
21				22	23	■	24			25	26	27
■	■	■	28			29	■	■	■	30		
31	32	33				■	34	35	36			
37			■	■	38				■	■	■	■
39			40	41	42	■	43			44	45	46
■	■	■	47			48		■	49			
50	51	52				■	53	54	■	55		
56				■	57				■	58		
59				■	60				■	61		

36 MORK & MINDY

1619 Pine Street, Boulder, Colorado

ACROSS

1 Cable network owned by AOL Time Warner
4 Door parts
9 *I've __ a Secret*
12 *The Facts of Life* star
13 Funny business
14 Yoko __
15 Compass point: Abbr.
16 Mindy portrayer
18 *Roots* character
20 58, in old Rome
21 *Chico __ the Man*
23 Ecology agency: Abbr.
24 Movie cable channel
27 Stare at
29 Opie's great-aunt
32 Mork portrayer
35 Sweet potato
36 Jeffreys of *Topper*
37 Johnson of *Laugh-In*
38 "__ Master's Voice" (RCA slogan)
39 Broken-down horse
41 TV studio sign
44 *Miami Vice* character
48 Mr. Bickley portrayer on the show
52 Auto Club letters
53 Wedding response
54 *Texaco Star Theater* star
55 Series that featured Eddie Murphy and Mike Myers: Abbr.
56 Draft agency: Abbr.
57 More frosty
58 Color

DOWN

1 *Star __: Deep Space Nine*
2 With 46 Down, Orkan farewell
3 MTV fan
4 *M*A*S*H* leave locale
5 __-Alicia of *Falcon Crest*
6 *Rhoda* production company
7 *The Price Is Right* action
8 Tool for Trapper John
9 Asian desert
10 "Dedicated to the __ Love"
11 Aaron Spelling's daughter
17 Wheeling's state: Abbr.
19 DeVito sitcom
22 Former *20/20* host
23 '90s sitcom
24 Use a skillet
25 Mauna __
26 Computer company
28 Rummy variety
29 Cheers, for one
30 CPR provider: Abbr.
31 Language suffix
33 __ Trio (Ernie Kovacs group)
34 *Othello* villain
38 In the know
40 *Lou Grant* star
41 Big name in elevators
42 Agrees silently
43 John of *Good Times*
45 __ *Bridges* (Don Johnson series)
46 See 2 Down
47 Jodie Foster alma mater
49 Minute fraction, for short
50 Prefix meaning "three"
51 Cheer for a toreador

A "bleem" was an Orkan time measure equal to 2,000 years.

Mork's all-purpose expletive was "Shazbot!"

The voice of Orson, Mork's Orkan superior, was provided by Ralph James.

37 MURPHY BROWN

CBS-TV, Washington, D.C.

ACROSS

1 *Here's Lucy* star
5 *Hawaii Five-O* star
9 Lab rodent
12 "I cannot tell __"
13 Spiny houseplant
14 In the past
15 Star of the show
18 Rush
19 Rock science: Abbr.
20 '50s kids series starring Peter Graves
21 Elation
22 Strange
24 The Galloping Gourmet, for example
27 Former airline
28 *Alice* spinoff
31 Faith Ford's role on the show
35 Large body of water
36 Former Cable TV award
37 *Our Gang* dog
38 ABC morning show initials
39 __ and haw
41 Diminutive suffix
44 Boxing results: Abbr.
46 Jack of *Barney Miller*
49 Network-president portrayer on the show
52 Day-__ paint
53 Dines
54 *The King* __
55 Wild blue yonder
56 Poker ritual
57 *Clarissa Explains It All* fan

DOWN

1 *The Dukes of Hazzard* actress
2 Jai __
3 Queue
4 Was in first place
5 Cagney's TV partner
6 Margarine
7 *The West Wing* star
8 Poor grade
9 The Big __ (*Laverne & Shirley* character)
10 Ripening agent
11 Mr. Danza
16 "__ to Extremes" (Billy Joel song)
17 *Mayberry* __
21 LBJ predecessor
23 Patriotic organization: Abbr.
24 Medicine dosages: Abbr.
25 Farm implement
26 Historical period
27 Common title starter
28 KAOS, to Smart
29 Great deal
30 Kind of poem
32 November vegetable
33 Crothers of *Chico and the Man*
34 Typing-speed abbreviation
38 From Berlin: Abbr.
39 Title character of 20 Across
40 Curved letter
41 Dairy products
42 Syndicated TV format
43 Actor Donahue
45 *The Greatest American Hero* star
46 Sensible
47 Ye __ Antique Shoppe
48 *thirtysomething* actor
50 Thumbs-up vote
51 Fedora, for instance

15 Across hired 93 different secretaries during the show's run.

The 93rd secretary, in the last episode, was portrayed by Bette Midler.

The local watering hole was Phil's.

38 THE ODD COUPLE

1049 Park Avenue, New York, New York

ACROSS

1 Soccer star Mia
5 Mail center: Abbr.
8 Frequent costume for Klinger
12 Brainstorm
13 Some MTV music
14 Miscellany
15 June 6, 1944
16 Atmosphere
17 Stare at
18 A star of the show
21 Telejournalist Wallace
22 Sing with closed mouth
23 French woman: Abbr.
24 Soup cooker
26 Like Fran Drescher's voice
30 Final or midterm
32 Integers: Abbr.
34 Use the microwave
35 Mrs. Carmichael, in *The Lucy Show*
37 Angry
39 *The __ Million Dollar Man*
40 __ Hill (San Francisco neighborhood)
42 *Laugh-In* cohost
44 A star of the show
48 Emollient ingredient
49 Suffix for press
50 Like a couch potato
53 Campbell of *Party of Five*
54 Sermon subject
55 High-schooler
56 Former spouses
57 Initials of FDR's successor
58 Looked at

DOWN

1 Made oneself scarce
2 Find a sum
3 *All in the Family* nickname
4 Barry Bostwick, in *Spin City*
5 Burt Ward's *Batman* role
6 Twosome
7 Big name in TV talk
8 *Roseanne* actor
9 Gymnast Korbut
10 Jean-Luc's second-in-command
11 Pet pig of Suzanne Sugarbaker
19 Edge out
20 '60s TV role for Sally Field
21 911, in Roman numerals
23 Kitten sound
25 Poston or Selleck
27 *L.A. Law* actress
28 Similar
29 *Smallville* character
31 Rock group in a '60s series
33 He succeeded Dick York in *Bewitched*
36 Chinese frypan
38 Mr. DeLuise
41 Magazine in *Just Shoot Me*
43 Ralph of *The Waltons*
44 Pauley or Curtin
45 Emcee Trebek
46 Crabapple __ (Hawkeye Pierce's hometown)
47 *Exodus* author
51 '50s kiddie host Pinky
52 The __

Felix's surname on the show was Unger; in the Broadway version, it was Ungar.

44 Across portrayed a sportswriter for the New York Herald.

18 Across' role was originated on Broadway by Art Carney.

39 OUR MISS BROOKS

Carroll Avenue, Madison, U.S.A.

ACROSS

1 Pitcher's infraction
5 Wooley of *Rawhide*
9 Did the catering for
12 Dentist's request
13 Julius Caesar garb
14 Bachelor's last words
15 Gale Gordon's role on the show
18 *Hazel* star
19 Brolin of *Marcus Welby, M.D.*
20 *The Streets of __ Francisco*
22 On the __ (exactly)
23 Barbara Walters' network
26 PBS talk-show host
28 "__ bigger than a breadbox?"
32 Walter Denton portrayer on the show
35 *Your Show of Shows* star
36 Polynesian carving
37 Fall behind
38 Speedometer reading: Abbr.
40 Patty Hearst's kidnappers: Abbr.
42 Burt Reynolds' *Gunsmoke* role
45 Author Jong
49 Biology teacher on the show
53 Bennett Cerf witticism
54 *Lois & Clark* star
55 Footnote notation
56 Start of a golf hole
57 Precipice
58 Start of a counting rhyme

DOWN

1 Inept sort
2 Lhasa __
3 Kids' block brand
4 Boy Scouts' expertise
5 Part of PST: Abbr.
6 Ad-__ committee
7 Part of the psyche
8 Instrument heard in the *Beverly Hillbillies* theme
9 Movie
10 Lou Grant's ex-wife
11 Johnson and Adams
16 Catherine of *SCTV*
17 Ms. Couric
21 Jay of *Dennis the Menace*
22 Cruise-ship levels
23 Curved line
24 Life story, for short
25 300, in old Rome
27 Reagan "Star Wars" program: Abbr.
29 NBC show produced by Lorne Michaels: Abbr.
30 __ moment (soon)
31 39 Down prop
33 *Hill Street Blues* actress
34 William Bendix TV role
39 *The __ Is Right*
41 *L.A. Law* character
42 Datebook entry: Abbr.
43 *Melrose Place* star
44 Evergreen tree
46 "Let __" (Beatles tune)
47 Nickel or dime
48 Rooney of *60 Minutes*
50 Writing tablet
51 *The __ Valley* (Stanwyck series)
52 Early afternoon

49 Across' (Robert Rockwell's) pet frog was Macdougal.

The pet cat of Connie Brooks' (Eve Arden's) landlady was Minerva.

The show's theme song was "Whistling Bells."

1	2	3	4		5	6	7	8		9	10	11
12					13					14		
15				16					17			
18							19					
			20		21		22					
23	24	25			26		27			28	29	30	31
32			33					34				
35					36					37		
			38	39			40		41			
42	43	44						45		46	47	48
49					50	51	52					
53					54					55		
56					57					58		

40 THE PARTRIDGE FAMILY

698 Sycamore Road, San Pueblo, California

ACROSS

1 Largest Internet service
4 *Married . . . __ Children*
8 Pre-__ student
11 Naval noncom: Abbr.
12 Resound
13 Keats poem
14 A star of the show
17 Skelton character Kadiddlehopper
18 "Who am __ say?"
19 Burbank clock setting: Abbr.
22 Byington of *December Bride*
27 __ Jima
30 Gobble up
32 Ms. O'Donnell
33 A star of the show
36 Hannibal Smith's men
37 *The __ From U.N.C.L.E.*
38 According to
39 *Full House* star
41 Cummings or Crane
43 Former Mideast nation: Abbr.
45 South Seas spot
49 A star of the show
54 Skirt edge
55 River of Spain
56 Switch positions
57 Bunny boss' nickname
58 Manuscript enclosure: Abbr.
59 Pursue romantically

DOWN

1 Electrically versatile
2 Whitish gemstone
3 __, *American Style* (*Happy Days* origin)
4 Get married
5 Truck-regulating agency: Abbr.
6 Asian cuisine
7 Alex Trebek and Bill Cullen
8 Miss Piggy pronoun
9 Byrnes of *77 Sunset Strip*
10 A star of the show
15 Dennis the Menace, for one
16 James Gandolfini TV role
20 *Dr. Quinn, Medicine Woman* star
21 Bar bill
23 Serling or Taylor
24 "The jig __!"
25 French Riviera resort
26 Will of *The Waltons*
27 Mrs. Morgenstern's namesakes
28 Light-bulb unit
29 Highest draft rating
31 Bergeron of *Hollywood Squares*
34 *China Beach* setting
35 Capture
40 Friend of White Fang and Black Tooth
42 Kitty Kelley book, for short
44 WB sitcom
46 Somers, on *Three's Company*
47 Letterman rival
48 Exxon's former name
49 "Be quiet!"
50 __ *Haw*
51 *Mission: Impossible* group: Abbr.
52 Many months: Abbr.
53 Mannix's first name

Mrs. Partridge's maiden name was Renfrew.

1	2	3	■	4	5	6	7	■	8	9	10	■
11			■	12				■	13			
14			15				■	16				
17				■		18		■				■
■	■		19	20	21		22	■	23	24	25	26
27	28	29	■	30		31		■	32			
33			34				35					
36				■	37			■	38			
39				40	■	41		42	■	■	■	■
■	■	■	43		44			■	45	46	47	48
■	49	50	51			52	53					
■	54			■	55			■	56			
■	57			■	58			■	59			

The local lovers' lane was Muldoon's Point.

The sign on the back of their bus:
CAREFUL, NERVOUS MOTHER DRIVING

41 THE PHIL SILVERS SHOW

Fort Baxter, Kansas

ACROSS

1 Neck of the woods
5 Creator of Mickey and Goofy
9 One of the Seven Dwarfs
12 *The Goldbergs* star
13 Bee Taylor's grand-nephew
14 G.I. hangout
15 *The Facts of Life* character
16 Sgt. Ritzik portrayer on the show
18 '20s auto
20 __-cone (summer treat)
21 CNN newsperson
24 *Diagnosis Murder* doctor
28 *60 Minutes* producer Hewitt
29 Explorer Vasco da __
33 Low-calorie, on labels
34 Harvey Lembeck's role on the show
37 Where Tulsa is: Abbr.
38 *Kraft Music Hall* host
39 Have a snack
40 *Austin Powers* portrayer
42 Jean of *Upstairs, Downstairs*
44 Hemisphere alliance: Abbr.
46 *Murder, She Wrote* network
47 Col. Hall portrayer on the show
51 Danny DeVito sitcom
55 Electrical unit
56 Author Wiesel
57 On the rocks
58 Brown shade
59 Top of a car
60 *The Untouchables* character

DOWN

1 *The Simpsons* grandpa
2 Mr. Skelton
3 Ending for north or west
4 Larry Storch sitcom role
5 *Barney Miller* character
6 Military address
7 Falsehoods
8 Freezing temperatures
9 The Dynamic __ (Batman and Robin)
10 CIA predecessor: Abbr.
11 Cliff Huxtable portrayer, familiarly
17 *Good Times* actress
19 Breakfast waffle name
21 Computer drive
22 Truant's offense
23 Fester, for one
25 Petroleum-filled ship
26 Book of maps
27 Poetic preposition
30 *World News Tonight* network
31 __ Tse-tung
32 Sweater part
35 *Brady Bunch* mom
36 Lemon of a show
41 Reporter Morley
43 *I'm Dickens, He's Fenster* star
45 Robert Vaughn TV role
46 Alphabetic quartet
47 Buttram of *Green Acres*
48 Doctors' org.
49 *Enterprise* network
50 __ de Janeiro
52 Expert
53 Crosses out
54 Passports, for instance: Abbr.

1	2	3	4		5	6	7	8		9	10	11
12					13					14		
15					16				17			
			18	19			20					
21	22	23						24		25	26	27
28				29	30	31	32		33			
34			35					36				
37				38					39			
40				41				42	43			
			44		45		46					
47	48	49				50			51	52	53	54
55				56					57			
58				59					60			

42 ROSEANNE

714 Delaware Street, Lanford, Illinois

ACROSS

1 Meriwether of *Barnaby Jones*
4 Zeppelin
9 Western scout Carson
12 Lawyers' group: Abbr.
13 Gary Burghoff sitcom role
14 Bride's response
15 Sara Gilbert's role on the show
18 Luke Perry's *90210* role
19 Robert Urich detective series
20 Actress Hagen
22 Near the ground
23 Clock part
26 Collarless shirts
28 Neptune's domain
31 Jackie Harris portrayer on the show
34 Cereal grain
35 Skating jump
36 Mr. Roarke, on *Fantasy Island*
37 The Matterhorn, for one
38 Hungry __ bear
40 Jetsons' dog
43 Kids' TV host of the '50s
47 Booker Brooks portrayer on the show
51 Inventor Whitney
52 Prefix for national
53 Hairstyling goo
54 Viscuso of *Soap*
55 Modern encyclopedia medium
56 Beer relative

DOWN

1 Cheryl of *Charlie's Angels*
2 Internet auction site
3 Holliman of *Police Woman*
4 Sportscaster Musburger
5 Office computer network: Abbr.
6 Chemical suffix
7 Big __ (Whopper alternative)
8 Jon of *Lassie*
9 *Scarecrow and Mrs. __*
10 Brainstorm
11 *Flipper* producer Ivan
16 Matt of *Today*
17 Contemporary
21 Devoured
22 Ms. Gibbons
23 *Alice* waitress
24 Road-service organization: Abbr.
25 Director's shout
27 Paramedic: Abbr.
28 __ Paulo, Brazil
29 Chicago trains
30 Toward the stern
32 Bane of Mr. Spock
33 Onetime *Hollywood Squares* regular
37 Part of ETA: Abbr.
39 *My Little Margie* star
40 Improves, as cheese
41 Ward of *Sisters*
42 Work hard
44 Actress Swenson
45 Diana Rigg TV role
46 Sitcom Marine
48 Finish
49 Middle: Abbr.
50 Sign of the zodiac

The original working title of the show was Life and Stuff.

The title character was employed as a waitress at the Lobo Lounge.

The family won $108 million in the Illinois State Lottery.

43 SANFORD AND SON

9114 South Central, Los Angeles, California

ACROSS

1 Banking convenience: Abbr.
4 '50s Korean conflict
7 __ Make a Deal
11 Where the buoys are
12 Yoko __
13 Morales of NYPD Blue
14 With "The," theme song of the show
17 Barbershop call
18 History-book chapter
19 Get up
23 Sally Jessy genre
27 Kind of camera: Abbr.
30 Computer "panic button"
31 Johnny __ (WKRP employee)
32 Overly
33 Liquid-Plumr competitor
35 Clock numeral
36 __ and dangerous
38 Superman foe Luthor
39 Prosecutors: Abbr.
40 Perused
41 Strong glue
43 Imitate
45 __ of the Century (game show)
49 A star of the show
54 Is obligated to
55 31 Across and colleagues
56 Pea case
57 Adam of Batman
58 Ambulance driver, often: Abbr.
59 Thoroughfares: Abbr.

DOWN

1 Trade organization: Abbr.
2 Head, in France
3 Duck Soup surname
4 Misfortune
5 Picnic crasher
6 Lowe or Reiner
7 Producer of the show
8 Silverstone on The Millionaire, for one
9 Menlo Park monogram
10 What Pyle called Carter
15 Greek letter
16 Shoe width
20 With 31 Down, a star of the show
21 Mideast nation: Abbr.
22 Top of the head
24 Enthusiastic
25 Star Wars princess
26 Cheryl Ladd, on Charlie's Angels
27 Sheriff-badge shape
28 Folk knowledge
29 Downey of Touched by an Angel
31 See 20 Down
34 Prefix meaning "new"
37 Daniel Boone actor
41 Poetic nighttime
42 Fashion monogram
44 Markie of Night Court
46 Poisonous snakes
47 Game-show winnings
48 Winds up
49 Leave It to Beaver star
50 Farm animal
51 Ike's initials
52 The Mary Tyler Moore Show station
53 Suffix meaning "adherent"

14 Across was written by Quincy Jones.

Pat Morita's role was Ah Chew.

The show was based on the British sitcom Steptoe and Son.

44 SEINFELD

129 West 81st Street, New York, New York

ACROSS

1 Wine-glass part
5 Soap ingredients
9 Blocker of *Bonanza*
12 Poet Angelou
13 *The Life and Legend of Wyatt __*
14 Mr. Romano
15 George Costanza portrayer on the show
17 Computer keyboard key
18 __ Grande
19 Feathery stole
20 Actress Brenneman
22 Dance for Morticia and Gomez
24 Archie's order to Edith
27 *Lou Grant* character
30 San __ Obispo, California
31 Otherwise
34 Had been
35 Egyptian crawlers
36 Location
37 ALF, for one
39 Mr. Magoo's first name
41 Laura Petrie portrayer
45 Thompson of *Caroline in the City*
46 Terre Haute school: Abbr.
48 __ and tuck
49 Bluto's would-be girlfriend
51 Hangout on the show
54 The Joker, to Batman
55 Neil Simon creation
56 Stack
57 Cat's covering
58 Hankerings
59 Mine rocks

DOWN

1 Don Adams role
2 Actress Shire
3 Keep an __ (watch)
4 *The Bionic Woman* dog
5 Carson successor
6 Conversation filler on the show
7 Poetic preposition
8 Lean eater of rhyme
9 Julia Louis-__ (a star of the show)
10 __ in "apple"
11 Setting of the show: Abbr.
16 Peek-__
21 Star of *Charmed*
23 Ben Cartwright portrayer
24 Emphatic agreement in Mexico
25 Part of the mouth
26 Superman's insignia
28 Rock gently
29 Actor Mineo
31 Lawyer's title: Abbr.
32 College in Brooklyn: Abbr.
33 Frank Costanza portrayer on the show
38 Australian birds
40 Like Cesar Romero as the Joker
42 TV studio sign
43 Lucas McCain's firearm
44 Fencing swords
46 __ instant (quickly)
47 "The __ the limit!"
49 Not operating
50 __ *Are There* ('50s documentary series)
52 Bullfight cheer
53 Sharkey's rank: Abbr.

15 Across' ATM password was "Bosco."

Jerry Seinfeld's favorite cereal was Double Crunch.

9 Down's employer was Pendant Publishing.

45 THE SIMPSONS

742 Evergreen Terrace, Springfield, U.S.A.

ACROSS

1 Marge, to Homer
5 Spielberg's first blockbuster
9 European airline
12 Elvis __ Presley
13 Dog in *Garfield*
14 Cheyenne's state: Abbr.
15 Lisa Simpson's instrument
17 Not feeling well
18 __ Francisco
19 Onetime movie reviewer on TV
21 Toll road: Abbr.
24 Words from the sponsor
26 "Little piggie"
27 That girl
28 Lab rodents
30 Gene Barry's first name on *Burke's Law*
33 Arizona neighbor
35 Allow
36 Alexandra of *Baywatch*
37 Karen Arnold on *The Wonder Years*
38 Votes in favor
40 Onetime owner of NBC
41 Fireplace residue
43 Actress Joanne
44 "Love __ neighbor"
45 *Nightline* host
48 Lawn condensation
50 Unit of current
51 Bart Simpson exclamation
56 Golf platform
57 Running gait
58 Virginia dance
59 Blow up a photo: Abbr.
60 Della Street portrayer
61 Plato of *Diff'rent Strokes*

DOWN

1 Existed
2 Nest-egg letters
3 *Spin City* star
4 *Dukes of Hazzard* character
5 *What's My Line?* host
6 Fuss
7 Finishes first
8 __ *Now* (Murrow documentary series)
9 Convenience store on the show
10 Waggoner of *Wonder Woman*
11 Bull Shannon portrayer
16 Carson predecessor
20 '70s Billy Crystal sitcom
21 Sound of dull impact
22 Wilson of *La Femme Nikita*
23 Bart Simpson's teacher
25 Patrick Macnee TV role
29 Start of a Picard log entry
31 "That hurts!"
32 Do in
34 Blair General, for one: Abbr.
39 Plaintiff
42 *The Big Valley* son
45 Shady Rest Hotel owner
46 Sign of the future
47 Northern constellation
49 Sela of *Sisters*
52 Major's superior: Abbr.
53 "Cry __ River"
54 One of the Walton kids
55 Mobile's state: Abbr.

Marge's maiden name is Bouvier.

1	2	3	4	■	5	6	7	8	■	9	10	11
12				■	13				■	14		
15				16					■	17		
■	■	■	18			■	19		20			
21	22	23	■	24		25	■	26			■	■
27			■	28			29	■	30		31	32
33		34	■	35			■	36				
37			■	38			39	■	40			
■	■	41		42		43			■	44		
45	46			■	47	■	48		49	■	■	■
50			■	51		52			■	53	54	55
56			■	57			■	58				
59			■	60			■	61				

Homer's bowling team is the Pin Pals.

The local seafood restaurant is the Rusty Barnacle.

46 3RD ROCK FROM THE SUN

417 Pensdale Drive, Rutherford, Ohio

ACROSS

1 Former Russian subdivision: Abbr.
4 Wharton degree: Abbr.
7 Sam Jaffe, on *Ben Casey*
12 Convenience store owner on *The Simpsons*
13 Large coffeemaker
14 Cable Ace, once
15 52 Across' role on the show
17 Tork of the Monkees
18 *One __ Beyond* (sci-fi series)
19 Arrest
21 __ a soul (no one)
22 Tyrannosaurus __
24 Letter after ar
26 Mr T's '80s group
29 Tourist's reference
30 Cat-eating alien
33 Title for 15 Across
36 Director Lee
37 Actor Wallach
38 Lisa Bonet's TV dad
39 Hawaiian souvenir
40 __ capita
41 New Age atmosphere
44 Shaq's league: Abbr.
46 Marshal McCloud's hometown
50 Stevens of *Peter Gunn*
52 A star of the show
54 Jessica Fletcher's home
55 Numero __
56 Prefix for center
57 Corby of *The Waltons*
58 Sixth sense: Abbr.
59 Concorde: Abbr.

DOWN

1 Backtalk
2 Commander Data's cat
3 Actress Janice
4 Silent
5 Setting of *The Goldbergs*
6 __ Maria Horsford of *Amen*
7 Use a ray gun
8 Bob Uecker, on *Mr. Belvedere*
9 Pro __ (proportionally)
10 __ Rabbit (Uncle Remus character)
11 "But it's __ heat" (summer rationalization)
16 Harpo Productions head
20 Smile broadly
23 Wink Martindale, for one
25 First word of the *Star Trek* introduction
26 Cry of discovery
27 Soft metal
28 Something to poach
29 2001, in old Rome
30 Words from the sponsor
31 Mideast nation: Abbr.
32 Use a skillet
34 Ken of *thirtysomething*
35 Compass point
39 Singer Frankie
40 *Growing __* (Thicke sitcom)
41 Wile E. Coyote's mail-order company
42 Russian river
43 Thin as a __
45 Union soldiers' color
47 Has another birthday
48 "How clumsy of me!"
49 Major Houlihan portrayer
51 Army bigwig: Abbr.
53 Apex

47 THREE'S COMPANY

Santa Monica, California

ACROSS

1 Compass point: Abbr.
4 Dame __ Everage
8 Germann of *Ally McBeal*
12 Rambo rescuee: Abbr.
13 Midday
14 Della's *Touched by an Angel* costar
15 __ Lanka
16 Landlord portrayer after Norman Fell
18 Prefix meaning "all"
20 Casting director's concerns
21 Tom Selleck TV role
23 *Chico and the Man* setting
27 Billy of *Father Knows Best*
29 __ *Garry Shandling's Show*
30 A star of the show
36 Clean-air agency: Abbr.
37 Thailand's former name
38 Cartwright of *The Danny Thomas Show*
42 *Jeopardy!* host
46 *Donahue* network
48 Put on the market
49 Joyce DeWitt's role on the show
53 __ Baba
54 Equitable
55 __ mater
56 Do wrong
57 Inger Stevens, on *The Farmer's Daughter*
58 Monica Geller's brother
59 "For shame!"

DOWN

1 __ salts
2 *The Wonder Years* mom
3 Larry Hagman TV role
4 Football position
5 Carlton, on *Rhoda*
6 Forbidden thing
7 Leg joint
8 Michael of *Family Ties*
9 Go bad
10 Paramedic: Abbr.
11 Helium or hydrogen
17 Teachers' union: Abbr.
19 Actress Swenson
22 Samovar
24 See 47 Down
25 Envelope contents: Abbr.
26 Burro
28 Thumbs-up vote
30 *Voyage to the Bottom of the* __
31 *Buffy the Vampire Slayer* network
32 Zig's partner
33 *Cheers* and *Happy Days*
34 Kayaker's need
35 French women: Abbr.
39 Ralph of *Nashville Now*
40 D-Day craft: Abbr.
41 Sadat of Egypt
43 Cruel one
44 Island for immigrants
45 Werner Klemperer TV role
47 With 24 Down, Texan's neckwear
49 Big Apple airport
50 Very narrow shoe
51 Prefix for picker
52 Prosecutors: Abbr.

Chrissy Snow's (30 Across') real first name was Christmas.

The neighbor-hood pub was the Regal Beagle.

Jack Tripper (John Ritter) worked as a chef at Angelino's Italian restaurant.

48 WELCOME BACK, KOTTER

34 Across High School, Brooklyn, New York

ACROSS

1 Hypo dosage: Abbr.
4 Chew like a beaver
8 __ Hogg (*Dukes of Hazzard* character)
12 Japanese drama
13 Numerical prefix
14 __ above (superior)
15 Freddie Washington's nickname on the show
17 Perlman of *Cheers*
18 *The People's Choice* dog
19 Prestigious TV award
21 The Waltons lived on one: Abbr.
24 Compass point: Abbr.
25 Peter Marshall's actress sister
28 Kentucky Jones, in a '60s series
30 Frasier's last name
34 High-school setting for the show
37 *Evening* __ (Reynolds sitcom)
38 Life science, for short
39 Hair coloring
40 Chowed down
42 Branch

44 Landon's wife on *Little House on the Prairie*
48 *Please Don't Eat the Daisies* surname
52 Be entitled to
53 Barbarino portrayer on the show
56 Cleveland's lake
57 __ podrida
58 __ *Miss Brooks*
59 Tail end
60 Doogie Howser portrayer __ Patrick Harris
61 Network owned by AOL

DOWN

1 *Wake-Up Call* network
2 Stylish
3 Where Agent 86's phone is
4 Sailor, slangily
5 Sergeant, for example: Abbr.
6 Perched upon
7 *Designing* __
8 *The Flintstones* producer
9 __ Rios, Jamaica
10 Took to court
11 Don't leave

16 Elyse Keaton or Maggie Seaver
20 Brokaw or Rather
22 Where sitcoms are watched
23 Omaha's state: Abbr.
25 WKRP employees: Abbr.
26 College cheer
27 Actress Thurman
29 Margarine holder
31 *McMillan __ Wife*
32 Roll-call vote
33 Compass point: Abbr.
35 Ted Knight's TV employer
36 Spy group: Abbr.
41 Sir __ John
43 Letters on a phone
44 Grandpa Walton portrayer
45 Very scarce
46 Opera solo
47 Author __ Stanley Gardner
49 Very much
50 Flabbergast
51 Roxanne of *Chicago Hope*
54 __ Baba
55 *Knots Landing* role

1	2	3	■	4	5	6	7	■	8	9	10	11
12			■	13				■	14			
15			16					■	17			
18				■		19		20				
■	■	■	21	22	23	■	24			■	■	■
25	26	27	■	28		29	■	30		31	32	33
34			35			36						
37				■	38			■	39			
■	■	■	40		41	■	42		43	■	■	■
44	45	46			■	47	■		48	49	50	51
52			■	53		54	55					
56			■	57			■		58			
59			■	60			■		61			

49 WKRP IN CINCINNATI

Flimm Building, Cincinnati, Ohio

ACROSS

1 Eve of *The Brady Bunch*
6 Family-room appliances
9 English telly initials
12 South Pacific island
13 "What a good boy __"
14 Battery size
15 Beatles drummer
16 A star of the show
18 Resourceful
20 *Growing Pains* star
21 John Steed portrayer
24 Military-law TV series
25 Long, long __
26 Chan's comment
28 Top-rated
32 Gordon Jump's role on the show
35 Japanese cooking ingredient
36 German article
37 __ polloi
38 Roofing material
40 Gilligan's home
42 Friend of Jim Rockford
45 Office assistant: Abbr.
46 Loni Anderson's role on the show
48 Tonoose, for one
52 Suffix for sugars
53 Solo of *Star Wars*
54 Dog on *Frasier*
55 Performers' union: Abbr.
56 Game-show host Fleming
57 Confiscate

DOWN

1 Letter addenda: Abbr.
2 Longitude opposite: Abbr.
3 Mrs. Ethan Hawke
4 24 Down portrayer
5 Adrienne of *Maude*
6 *Soap* surname
7 Southern military school: Abbr.
8 Carol Kane, on *Taxi*
9 Jethro Bodine portrayer
10 *Mission: Impossible* actress
11 Ill-mannered men
17 Fit for a queen
19 PBS anchorman
21 Address often used by Joe Friday
22 Farming prefix
23 Portable beds
24 *Happy Days* character
27 Mr. Wizard's specialty: Abbr.
29 Workplace-safety agency: Abbr.
30 Popular lunchtime
31 City in Oklahoma
33 '80s James Brolin series
34 Police drama plot lines
39 McGarrett's farewell
41 Onetime *Hollywood Squares* regular
42 Grandpa McCoy
43 *I Dream of Jeannie* organization
44 Dharma's hubby
45 Mailed away
47 Armed conflict
49 401, in Roman numerals
50 *Room 222* teacher
51 Shoe width

50 THE WONDER YEARS

Anytown, U.S.A.

ACROSS

1 Crow sound
4 Encouraging word
8 Catherine of *The Dukes of Hazzard*
12 Inventor Whitney
13 Actress Olin
14 *The Time Machine* race
15 Mr. Skelton
16 U.N.C.L.E. employees: Abbr.
17 Network division
18 A star of the show
21 Mt. St. Helens output
22 *Six Million Dollar Man* boss
26 Study hard
29 "Ignorance of the law __ excuse"
32 Out __ limb
33 Junior high attended by Kevin Arnold
36 Exploit
37 Jacob's twin
38 Lou Grant's ex
39 *The Many Loves of Dobie Gillis* girl
41 Adversity
43 A star of the show
49 Donna Mills, on *Knots Landing*
52 Benedict of *The A-Team*
53 Salesperson
54 Petersen of *The Donna Reed Show*
55 Suffix for kitchen
56 Skater Babilonia
57 Computer-storage unit
58 Oohs and __
59 Compass point: Abbr.

DOWN

1 *What's My Line?* punster
2 Oriole or Mariner
3 ABC's __ *World of Sports*
4 *Head of the __* (Hesseman sitcom)
5 *M*A*S*H* and *All in the Family*, for example
6 Being broadcast
7 Space shuttle agency
8 *Seinfeld* character
9 British brew
10 Eleanor on *Green Acres*
11 That guy's
19 Title for Diana Rigg
20 Hoodlum
23 Like some dorms
24 "__ Love Her" (Beatles tune)
25 Portrayer of Mel's mother on *Alice*
26 Brandon of *The Courtship of Eddie's Father*
27 Betty White, on *The Golden Girls*
28 Cain's brother
30 Jamaican music
31 *Cheers* actress
34 __ *People* (Sarah Purcell series)
35 Have to have
40 Bosley on *Charlie's Angels*
42 Randi of *CHiPs*
44 Notion
45 *La Dolce __* (Fellini film)
46 Johnson of *Laugh-In*
47 Game-show panelist Orson
48 Ronny Howard role
49 Police alert: Abbr.
50 Workplace for Mitch Bucannon
51 However

1	2	3		4	5	6	7		8	9	10	11
12				13					14			
15				16					17			
18			19					20				
			21					22		23	24	25
26	27	28			29	30	31			32		
33				34					35			
36				37					38			
39			40				41	42				
			43		44	45				46	47	48
49	50	51			52					53		
54					55					56		
57					58					59		

MORE EXCITING AND CHALLENGING
TITLES BY STANLEY NEWMAN

VOL.	ISBN	QUAN.	PRICE	TOTAL
BY STANLEY NEWMAN				
Stanley Newman's Coffee Time Word Games				
	0812934539	___	$7.95	___
Random House Golf Crosswords				
	0812933966	___	$6.95	___
Stanley Newman's Literary Crosswords: Something Novel				
	0812935047	___	$8.95	___
Stanley Newman's Movie Mania Crosswords				
	0812934687	___	$7.95	___
Stanley Newman's Sitcom Crosswords				
	0812934695	___	$7.95	___
New York Times Square One Crossword Puzzle Dictionary				
by Stanley Newman and Daniel Stark				
	0812930436	___	$23.00	___
10,000 Answers: The Ultimate Trivia Encyclopedia				
by Stanley Newman and Hal Fittipaldi				
	037571944X	___	$24.95	___
Stanley Newman's Sunday Crosswords				
Vol. 1	0812934512	___	$9.95	___
Vol. 2	0812935144	___	$9.95	___
Random House Back to the Beach Crosswords				
	0812934768	___	$6.95	___
Random House Bedtime Crosswords				
	0812934679	___	$6.95	___
Random House By the Fireside Crosswords				
	0812934199	___	$6.95	___
Random House Cabin Fever Crosswords				
	0812934776	___	$6.95	___
Random House Cozy Crosswords				
	0812934326	___	$6.95	___

VOL.	ISBN	QUAN.	PRICE	TOTAL
Random House Spring Training Crosswords				
	0812934784	___	$6.95	___
Random House Summer Vacation Crosswords				
	0812934792	___	$6.95	___
Random House Vacation Crosswords				
	0812932897	___	$6.95	___
Random House More Vacation Crosswords				
	0812934180	___	$6.95	___
EDITED BY STANLEY NEWMAN				
Random House Sunday Crosswords				
Vol. 1	0812925548	___	$9.95	___
Vol. 7	0812934164	___	$9.95	___
Random House Club Crosswords				
Edited by Stanley Newman and Mel Rosen				
Vol. 1	0812926382	___	$13.95	___
Vol. 2	081292892X	___	$13.95	___
Vol. 3	0812929691	___	$13.95	___
Vol. 4	0812931246	___	$13.00	___
Vol. 5	0812932900	___	$13.00	___
Random House Sunday Crossword Omnibus				
Vol. 1	0812933982	___	$12.95	___
Random House Monster Sunday Crossword Omnibus				
Vol. 1	0812930592	___	$17.50	___
Random House Monster Crossword Puzzle Omnibus				
Vol. 1	0812932137	___	$17.50	___
Random House Mammoth Crossword Puzzle Omnibus				
	081293394X	___	$16.95	___
Random House UltraHard Crossword Omnibus				
Vol. 1	0812931262	___	$12.50	___
Random House Masterpiece Crosswords Collection				
	0812934946	___	$12.95	___

1

```
OGLE  DEAL   PAT
SOOT  AXLE   UMA
COUSINITT    GYM
ASI   FAT  BUS
REEDS     GELLAR
      WOODY  LENA
MAYA  UAR   MYTH
TROY  RHODA
SKUNKS     ANNIE
    REO  CAT  IND
SPA   JOHNASTIN
HEN   ALIT  GENA
EGG   KANE  TSKS
```

2

```
WILT   AID   GRAS
AFOR   DNA   RISK
DAVIDANDRICKY
STEVE      UMASS
       ILL  PLY
RHEA   ERLE  SAO
HOLLYWOODHIGH
OWL    AINT  ITEM
       CCS   SST
ALLAH        THREE
FOURTEENYEARS
ASTO   NAB   RUMP
REEL   ETC   ELAN
```

3

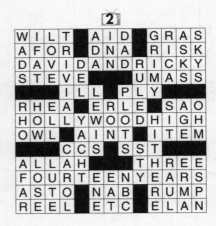
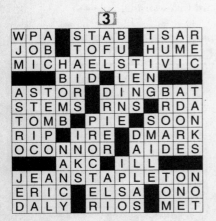

```
WPA   STAB   TSAR
JOB   TOFU   HUME
MICHAELSTIVIC
      BID   LEN
ASTOR     DINGBAT
STEMS  RNS   RDA
TOMB   PIE   SOON
RIP    IRE   DMARK
OCONNOR     AIDES
      AKC   ILL
JEANSTAPLETON
ERIC   ELSA  ONO
DALY   RIOS  MET
```

4

```
LAD   AWLS   MAMA
ALI   RHEA   OPED
RON   DONKNOTTS
STONE       EAR
       ENDS  REESE
ALDA   CLAD  ROT
NORTHCAROLINA
TBA    ALTA  INST
IOWAN  ETAS
       RNA   NANNY
JIMNABORS   ADO
IDEA   ELMO  BAG
FONZ   TENN  SKI
```

5

```
MASH  ECO    SIAM
AIRE  DIP    ARTE
CLAMPETT     GEOG
       SONY  DANZA
CABLE       DALE
BLUE   ALAN  RAM
EDGY   MAY   TYNE
RAT    ROSS  OATS
       USES  ANNES
CBSTV      GARY
ELSE   DRYSDALE
RULE   EEE   OWES
FRED   NYS   WEST
```

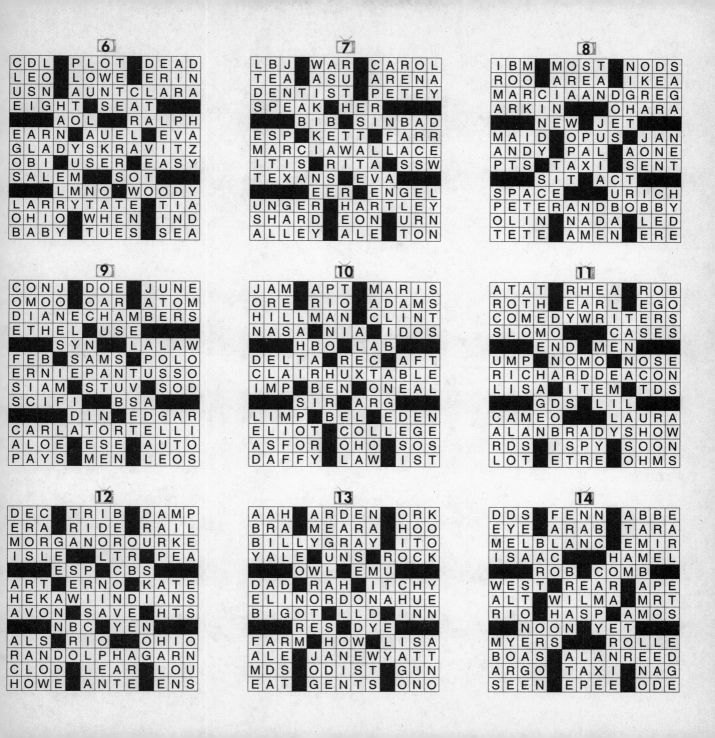

15

```
C T S . P R S . S H O R E
N R A . A H A . W O R K S
B U L L D O G . E U R O S
C E S A R . A M E N . . .
. . . N E B . U P D A T E
S M E E . R A R E . I R A
K E L S E Y G R A M M E R
Y A M . N A T O . A S K S
E N S I G N . W A R . . .
. . . B L T S . C L A R K
L O T S A . M A H O N E Y
S O R E N . O L E . K E R
U P A N D . G A S . A K A
```

16

```
P H A T . T R I B . C A T
O A T H . B O N O . A S H
T Y R A B A N K S . R A Y
T E E N A . Y O W L . . .
S S E . S O L . M I T C H
. . . V E N U S . D O P E
D A N A . E C O . O N A N
O D I N . L A L A W . . .
C O A C H . S O D . B U M
. . . L E O N . D A R L A
G O O . W I L L S M I T H
N U N . D C I I . A C R E
P I G . Y E L P . N E A R
```

17

```
S S T S . O D D . W A S
I H O P . N O R . A R I
M O N I C A G E L L E R
P O K E R . S W A T . .
. . . S A M . P E A C E
T A C . I A S K . R Y A N
E L I . G R E E N . E G O
A D A M . K E R I . S Y S
M O O S E . R E W . . .
. . . Q U I Z . C H A S E
C O U R T E N E Y C O X
A N A . T R I . M I L E
R O D . O O P . E D D S
```

18

```
M U I R . T E A M . C B S
O S L O . A G R A . O A R
M E L B R O O K S . N I A
. . . O H S . O W E N S
T O N T O . C A N I . . .
U N E . D O L L . L I R A
B A R B A R A F E L D O N
A N D Y . B R A D . O R K
. . . T R E K . I L L Y A
V I D E O . S T E . . .
E R A . B U C K H E N R Y
R O Y . I S P Y . Z O O S
A N S . N C O S . A W O L
```

19

```
M A R X . J U L . A D E S
C H E F . U S A . S A L A
S S M I N N O W . T W O S
. . . L I E . A R N I E
G O B E L . A R R O W . .
E N O S . S L O T . E E R
N A B . T O O L S . L S U
E N D . W A H L . G L A D
. . . E R I K A . R O S I E
C O N A N . G A P . . .
E N V S . A L A N H A L E
S T E P . B U B . E D I E
T O R Y . A C E . R O L E
```

20

```
H B O . Y O G A . T U F T
O A K . A R M S . I G L U
S C I . B E A A R T H U R
T H E W B . . . O L S E N
. . . H A N . A W E . . .
B O Z O . I O W A . A B C
R U E M C C L A N A H A N
A T E . R O A R . Z A H N
. . . O I L . D R U . . .
C R A N E . O R B I T
D E V E R E A U X . A D A
E L I A . T O R I . R E X
F O A M . A L I E . T A I
```

21

```
P O L . M A Y . Z E L D A
A K A . I W O . O N E A L
M R H A N E Y . R E E S E
S A R G E . O E R . . .
. . . E R R . N O R M A N
C D E . V O I D . P O L E
L I S A A N D O L I V E R
A S S T . N O R A . E C O
W H O O P I . A W L . . .
. . . E E E . S A F E R
S U S A N . D O U G L A S
A S T I N . N O I . I R V
P E R R Y . A P T . T S P
```

22

```
M C D . A S K . M A R L O
A H A . N R A . O L E O S
S I T O N I T . R A L P H
S P A N . E T S . Y E A
. . . A S H . H E F . . .
D D E . S A D A . B E E P
A N S O N W I L L I A M S
M A C Y . A M I D . T U T
. . . L E I . A L I . . .
G P O . L I T . N A N U
H E N R Y . W I N K L E R
I T E M S . I D O . B I G
J E S S E . N A W . A L E
```

23

```
S N U B . J O E . M G M T
P E R U . A H S . E E E E
A U D R E Y M E A D O W S
S T U B S . . . M I L L S
. . . A S S . B B C . . .
D E A N . T A I L . A N D
J A C K I E G L E A S O N
S U E . R E E K . Y A D A
. . . F E D . O R K . . .
A L L A N . F R O S T
J O Y C E R A N D O L P H
A B E T . I K E . Y E A R
R O S S . P A T . D O M O
```

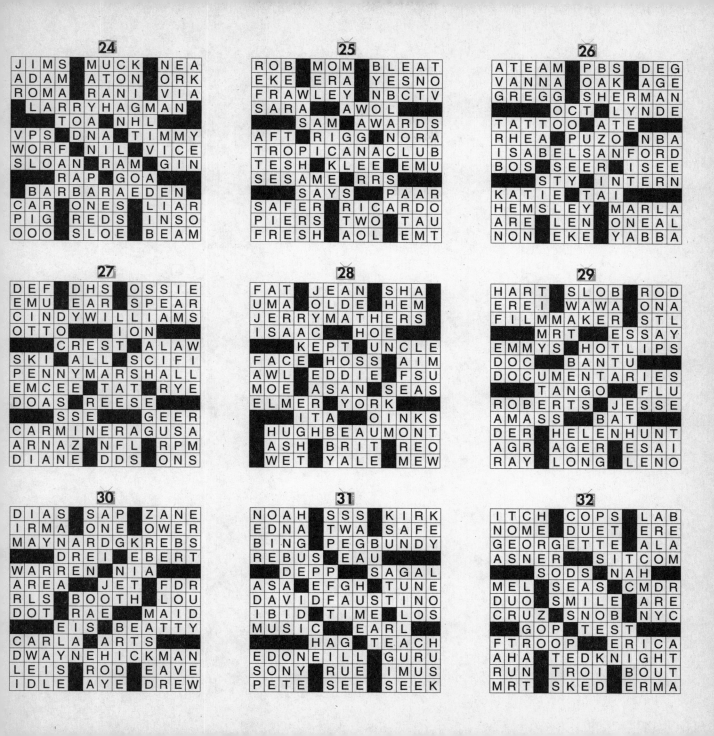

24

```
JIMS  MUCK  NEA
ADAM  ATON  ORK
ROMA  RANI  VIA
 LARRYHAGMAN
   TOA  NHL
VPS  DNA  TIMMY
WORF  NIL  VICE
SLOAN  RAM  GIN
   RAP  GOA
 BARBARAEDEN
CAR  ONES  LIAR
PIG  REDS  INSO
OOO  SLOE  BEAM
```

25

```
ROB  MOM  BLEAT
EKE  ERA  YESNO
FRAWLEY  NBCTV
SARA   AWOL
   SAM  AWARDS
AFT  RIGG  NORA
TROPICANACLUB
TESH  KLEE  EMU
SESAME  RRS
   SAYS  PAAR
SAFER  RICARDO
PIERS  TWO  TAU
FRESH  AOL  EMT
```

26

```
ATEAM  PBS  DEG
VANNA  OAK  AGE
GREGG  SHERMAN
    OCT  LYNDE
TATTOO  ATE
RHEA  PUZO  NBA
ISABELSANFORD
BOS  SEER  ISEE
   STY  INTERN
KATIE  TAI
HEMSLEY  MARLA
ARE  LEN  ONEAL
NON  EKE  YABBA
```

27

```
DEF  DHS  OSSIE
EMU  EAR  SPEAR
CINDYWILLIAMS
OTTO   ION
   CREST  ALAW
SKI  ALL  SCIFI
PENNYMARSHALL
EMCEE  TAT  RYE
DOAS  REESE
   SSE  GEER
CARMINERAGUSA
ARNAZ  NFL  RPM
DIANE  DDS  ONS
```

28

```
FAT  JEAN  SHA
UMA  OLDE  HEM
JERRYMATHERS
ISAAC  HOE
   KEPT  UNCLE
FACE  HOSS  AIM
AWL  EDDIE  FSU
MOE  ASAN  SEAS
ELMER  YORK
   ITA  OINKS
HUGHBEAUMONT
ASH  BRIT  REO
WET  YALE  MEW
```

29

```
HART  SLOB  ROD
EREI  WAWA  ONA
FILMMAKER  STL
   MRT  ESSAY
EMMYS  HOTLIPS
DOC   BANTU
DOCUMENTARIES
   TANGO  FLU
ROBERTS  JESSE
AMASS   BAT
DER  HELENHUNT
AGR  AGER  ESAI
RAY  LONG  LENO
```

30

```
DIAS  SAP  ZANE
IRMA  ONE  OWER
MAYNARDGKREBS
   DREI  EBERT
WARREN  NIA
AREA  JET  FDR
RLS  BOOTH  LOU
DOT  RAE  MAID
   EIS  BEATTY
CARLA  ARTS
DWAYNEHICKMAN
LEIS  ROD  EAVE
IDLE  AYE  DREW
```

31

```
NOAH  SSS  KIRK
EDNA  TWA  SAFE
BING  PEGBUNDY
REBUS  EAU
   DEPP  SAGAL
ASA  EFGH  TUNE
DAVIDFAUSTINO
IBID  TIME  LOS
MUSIC  EARL
   HAG  TEACH
EDONEILL  GURU
SONY  RUE  IMUS
PETE  SEE  SEEK
```

32

```
ITCH  COPS  LAB
NOME  DUET  ERE
GEORGETTE  ALA
ASNER  SITCOM
   SODS  NAH
MEL  SEAS  CMDR
DUO  SMILE  ARE
CRUZ  SNOB  NYC
   GOP  TEST
FTROOP  ERICA
AHA  TEDKNIGHT
RUN  TROI  BOUT
MRT  SKED  ERMA
```

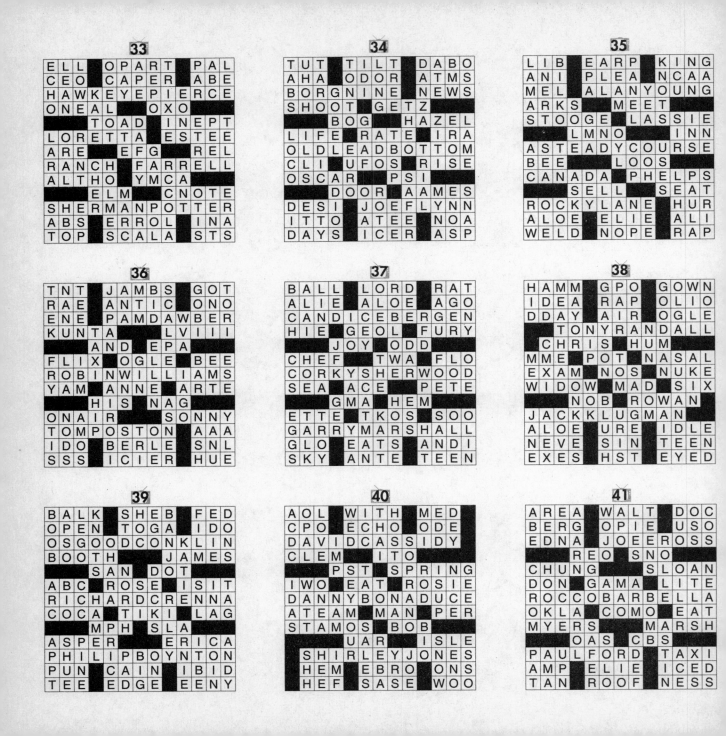

33

E	L	L			O	P	A	R	T		P	A	L	
C	E	O		C	A	P	E	R			A	B	E	
H	A	W	K	E	Y	E	P	I	E	R	C	E		
O	N	E	A	L				O	X	O				
			T	O	A	D			I	N	E	P	T	
L	O	R	E	T	T	A			E	S	T	E	E	
A	R	E			E	F	G			R	E	L		
R	A	N	C	H		F	A	R	R	E	L	L		
A	L	T	H	O		Y	M	C	A					
			E	L	M			C	N	O	T	E		
S	H	E	R	M	A	N	P	O	T	T	E	R		
A	B	S			E	R	R	O	L		I	N	A	
T	O	P		S	C	A	L	A			S	T	S	

34

T	U	T		T	I	L	T		D	A	B	O
A	H	A		O	D	O	R		A	T	M	S
B	O	R	G	N	I	N	E		N	E	W	S
S	H	O	O	T		G	E	T	Z			
			B	O	G			H	A	Z	E	L
L	I	F	E		R	A	T	E		I	R	A
O	L	D	L	E	A	D	B	O	T	T	O	M
C	L	I		U	F	O	S		R	I	S	E
O	S	C	A	R		P	S	I				
			D	O	O	R		A	A	M	E	S
D	E	S	I		J	O	E	F	L	Y	N	N
I	T	T	O		A	T	E	E		N	O	A
D	A	Y	S		I	C	E	R		A	S	P

35

L	I	B		E	A	R	P		K	I	N	G
A	N	I		P	L	E	A		N	C	A	A
M	E	L		A	L	A	N	Y	O	U	N	G
A	R	K	S			M	E	E	T			
S	T	O	O	G	E		L	A	S	S	I	E
			L	M	N	O				I	N	N
A	S	T	E	A	D	Y	C	O	U	R	S	E
B	E	E				L	O	O	S			
C	A	N	A	D	A		P	H	E	L	P	S
		S	E	L	L				S	E	A	T
R	O	C	K	Y	L	A	N	E		H	U	R
A	L	O	E		E	L	I	E		A	L	I
W	E	L	D		N	O	P	E		R	A	P

36

T	N	T		J	A	M	B	S		G	O	T
R	A	E		A	N	T	I	C		O	N	O
E	N	E		P	A	M	D	A	W	B	E	R
K	U	N	T	A			L	V	I	I	I	
			A	N	D		E	P	A			
F	L	I	X		O	G	L	E		B	E	E
R	O	B	I	N	W	I	L	L	I	A	M	S
Y	A	M		A	N	N	E		A	R	T	E
			H	I	S		N	A	G			
O	N	A	I	R				S	O	N	N	Y
T	O	M	P	O	S	T	O	N		A	A	A
I	D	O		B	E	R	L	E		S	N	L
S	S	S		I	C	I	E	R		H	U	E

37

B	A	L	L		L	O	R	D		R	A	T
A	L	I	E		A	L	O	E		A	G	O
C	A	N	D	I	C	E	B	E	R	G	E	N
H	I	E		G	E	O	L		F	U	R	Y
			J	O	Y		O	D	D			
C	H	E	F			T	W	A		F	L	O
C	O	R	K	Y	S	H	E	R	W	O	O	D
S	E	A		A	C	E		P	E	T	E	
			G	M	A		H	E	M			
E	T	T	E		T	K	O	S		S	O	O
G	A	R	R	Y	M	A	R	S	H	A	L	L
G	L	O		E	A	T	S		A	N	D	I
S	K	Y		A	N	T	E		T	E	E	N

38

H	A	M	M		G	P	O		G	O	W	N
I	D	E	A		R	A	P		O	L	I	O
D	D	A	Y		A	I	R		O	G	L	E
			T	O	N	Y	R	A	N	D	A	L	L
		C	H	R	I	S		H	U	M		
M	M	E		P	O	T		N	A	S	A	L
E	X	A	M		N	O	S		N	U	K	E
W	I	D	O	W		M	A	D		S	I	X
			N	O	B		R	O	W	A	N	
J	A	C	K	K	L	U	G	M	A	N		
A	L	O	E		U	R	E		I	D	L	E
N	E	V	E		S	I	N		T	E	E	N
E	X	E	S		H	S	T		E	Y	E	D

39

B	A	L	K		S	H	E	B		F	E	D
O	P	E	N		T	O	G	A		I	D	O
O	S	G	O	O	D	C	O	N	K	L	I	N
B	O	O	T	H				J	A	M	E	S
			S	A	N		D	O	T			
A	B	C		R	O	S	E		I	S	I	T
R	I	C	H	A	R	D	C	R	E	N	N	A
C	O	C	A		T	I	K	I		L	A	G
			M	P	H		S	L	A			
A	S	P	E	R				E	R	I	C	A
P	H	I	L	I	P	B	O	Y	N	T	O	N
P	U	N		C	A	I	N		I	B	I	D
T	E	E		E	D	G	E		E	E	N	Y

40

A	O	L		W	I	T	H		M	E	D
C	P	O		E	C	H	O		O	D	E
D	A	V	I	D	C	A	S	S	I	D	Y
C	L	E	M		I	T	O				
			P	S	T		S	P	R	I	N	G
I	W	O		E	A	T		R	O	S	I	E
D	A	N	N	Y	B	O	N	A	D	U	C	E
A	T	E	A	M		M	A	N		P	E	R
S	T	A	M	O	S		B	O	B			
			U	A	R			I	S	L	E	
S	H	I	R	L	E	Y	J	O	N	E	S	
H	E	M		E	B	R	O		O	N	S	
H	E	F		S	A	S	E		W	O	O	

41

A	R	E	A		W	A	L	T		D	O	C
B	E	R	G		O	P	I	E		U	S	O
E	D	N	A		J	O	E	E	R	O	S	S
			R	E	O			S	N	O		
C	H	U	N	G				S	L	O	A	N
D	O	N		G	A	M	A		L	I	T	E
R	O	C	C	O	B	A	R	B	E	L	L	A
O	K	L	A		C	O	M	O		E	A	T
M	Y	E	R	S				M	A	R	S	H
			O	A	S		C	B	S			
P	A	U	L	F	O	R	D		T	A	X	I
A	M	P		E	L	I	E		I	C	E	D
T	A	N		R	O	O	F		N	E	S	S

42

```
LEE  BLIMP KIT
ABA  RADAR IDO
DARLENECONNER
DYLAN   VEGAS
  UTA LOW
FACE TEES SEA
LAURIEMETCALF
OAT LUTZ HOST
  ALP ASA
ASTRO   TRIPP
GEORGECLOONEY
ELI INTER GEL
SAL CDROM ALE
```

43

```
ATM WAR  LETS
SEA ONO  ESAI
STREETBEATER
NEXT   ERA
  ARISE TALK
SLR ESC FEVER
TOO DRANO III
ARMED LEX DAS
READ EPOXY
  APE  SALE
DEMONDWILSON
OWES DJS POD
WEST EMT STS
```

44

```
STEM LYES DAN
MAYA EARP RAY
ALEXANDER ESC
RIO BOA AMY
TANGO  STIFLE
   ROSSI LUIS
ELSE WAS ASPS
SITE ALIEN
QUINCY  MOORE
  LEA ISU NIP
OYL MONKSCAFE
FOE PLAY PILE
FUR YENS ORES
```

45

```
WIFE JAWS KLM
ARON ODIE WYO
SAXOPHONE ILL
  SAN SISKEL
TPK ADS TOE
HER RATS AMOS
UTAH LET PAUL
DABO YEAS RCA
 ASH DRU THY
KOPPEL DEW
AMP AYCARAMBA
TEE TROT REEL
ENL HALE DANA
```

46

```
SSR MBA ZORBA
APU URN AWARD
SOLOMON PETER
STEP NAB NARY
  REX ESS
ATEAM MAP ALF
HIGHCOMMANDER
ANG ELI COSBY
  LEI PER
AURA NBA TAOS
CRAIG LITHGOW
MAINE UNO EPI
ELLEN ESP SST
```

47

```
ENE EDNA GREG
POW NOON ROMA
SRI DONKNOTTS
OMNI ROLES
MAGNUM EASTLA
  GRAY   ITS
SUZANNESOMERS
EPA  SIAM
ANGELA TREBEK
  MSNBC SELL
JANETWOOD ALI
FAIR ALMA SIN
KATY ROSS TSK
```

48

```
CCS GNAW BOSS
NOH OCTO ACUT
BOOMBOOM RHEA
CLEO PEABODY
  MTN NNE
DRU VET CRANE
JAMESBUCHANAN
SHADE BIO DYE
  ATE ARM
GRASSLE NASH
EARN TRAVOLTA
ERIE OLLA OUR
REAR NEIL TNT
```

49

```
PLUMB TVS BBC
SAMOA AMI AAA
STARR TIMREID
  ABLE KERNS
MACNEE JAG
AGO AHSO AONE
ARTHURCARLSON
MISO EINE HOI
  TAR ISLAND
ANGEL SECY
MARLOWE UNCLE
OSE HAN EDDIE
SAG ART SEIZE
```

50

```
CAW CMON BACH
ELI LENA ELOI
RED AGTS NEWS
FREDSAVAGE
  ASH  OSCAR
CRAM ISNO ONA
ROBERTKENNEDY
USE ESAU EDIE
ZELDA  WOE
  OLIVIADABO
ABBY DIRK REP
PAUL ETTE TAI
BYTE AAHS ENE
```